BURN THIS BOOK

*What Keith Ellison Doesn't Want
You to Know About His Radical
Marxist/Islamist Associations and Agenda*

By

Trevor Loudon

21 August 2018

For more information about this book, visit
SECUREFREEDOM.ORG

Burn This Book
is published in the United States
by the Center for Security Policy Press,
a division of the Center for Security Policy.

ISBN-13: 978-1726030298
ISBN-10: 1726030296

The Center for Security Policy
Washington, D.C.
Phone: 202-835-9077
Email: info@SecureFreedom.org
For more information, visit SecureFreedom.org

Interior design by Bravura Books

*"We oftentimes had these debates and discussions about 'out of the streets and into the suites'—that was the term that was used to describe the swan song of the civil rights movement. ... He made a decision and thought **he could make a difference by being on the inside**."* [emphasis added]

— Socialist Workers Party member and University of Minnesota Professor August Nimtz on longtime friend Keith Ellison

Table of Contents

Foreword 1

Chapter One: Who Is Keith Ellison? 5

Chapter Two: Conversion to Islam 9

Chapter Three: All In With the Hard Left 15

Chapter Four: The Legal Rights Center 27

Chapter Five: Rainbow Politics and 'Being on the Inside' 35

Chapter Six: Out with the Communists, In With Democratic Socialists of America 43

Chapter Seven: Back in the Fold of Orthodox Sunni Islam 57

Chapter Eight: Straddling the Radical Left and the Islamic Movement 69

Chapter Nine: 'Enemies foreign and domestic …' 77

Appendix A: Keith Ellison: Speaking Engagements with Muslim Brotherhood Front Organizations 81

Appendix B: Contributions to Rep. Keith Ellison 2006-2017 85

References 101

Index 115

Foreword

On July 17, 2018, Representative Keith Ellison of Minnesota wrote Amazon CEO Jeffrey Bezos, demanding that his company censor books and other products by those deemed to be "hate groups" by the discredited Southern Poverty Law Center. He called for such materials still in Amazon warehouses to be "destroyed" over the next three months and an end to the company's publication of similar "physical and digital materials."

There is reason to believe that you are reading the impetus behind Keith Ellison's call for book burning. In the course of a July 3rd interview with author Diana West on our nationally syndicated "Secure Freedom Radio" program, I mentioned that we would shortly publish a book about the Congressman's ominous past and present ties to Marxist and Islamist groups and their agendas. Since the hard left monitors our show assiduously, word of this publication may well have reached Mr. Ellison before the 17th. And, as the Center for Security Policy Press uses Amazon's CreateSpace service to publish its many monographs and books, censoring such works – past, as well as future – could prevent readers from seeing this one.

That is because the Center for Security Policy is one of the organizations the discredited Southern Poverty Law Center (SPLC)[1] has falsely characterized as a "hate group." By pressing Amazon's Bezos to use the SPLC as the arbiter of what content can be published or maintained in inventory, Rep. Ellison could achieve the censorship of CSP's products without spedifying us as the target.

As this book by Trevor Loudon amply demonstrates, such stealthy subversiveness is the stock-in-trade of Keith Ellison. His associations dating back to his involvement with the Nation of

---

[1] The SPLC recently paid over $3 million for falsely labeling someone an "anti-Muslim extremist." This settlement amounts to an acknowledgment that the organization's research is unreliable and causes material damage to those it wrongly smears.

Islam as a student at Wayne State University and continuing to his present—and ongoing—involvement with Muslim Brotherhood fronts and his role as chairman of the radical House Progressive Caucus, Keith Ellison's record is one of unbroken ties to extremists committed to subverting our country.

This insight is all the more alarming in light of a dangerously mistaken, but widespread assumption: When an elected official in the United States swears an oath to defend the U.S. Constitution against all enemies foreign and domestic, they are presumed to be truthfully saying they are able and willing to do that. Consequently, such representatives of the American people in the U.S. Congress are not subjected to the sort of background investigations aimed at confirming that assumption that is required of, for example, postal employees, securities personnel and school bus drivers.

Unfortunately, as author, filmmaker and national security expert Trevor Loudon documents exhaustively in this volume, Rep. Keith Ellison's many and longstanding personal associations with groups openly hostile to the principles and even the existence of the U.S. Constitution, would likely make it impossible for him to to pass even the most cursory of security checks.

Highlights of Mr. Loudon's carefully cited research into Rep. Ellison's personal involvement with openly anti-American individuals and organizations include the following:

- During Keith Ellison's college years, he was drawn to communism and radical leftist causes. His connections with Maoist and Trotskyist activists persist to this day.

- At Wayne State, Ellison also began to associate with the viciously antisemitic, racist Nation of Islam. While, as a candidate for public office, he later claimed to regret such ties, he has from time to time continued them.

- He has supported liberalized American travel to Communist Cuba and convicted felon Bernadine Dohrn of the revolutionary Weather Underground.

- Keith Ellison was endorsed and abetted by the Minnesota Communist Party and Democratic Socialists of America when he ran for Congress.

- His campaign received strong support from the Somali refugee community in Minneapolis, among the most unassimilated and aggressively Sharia-supremacist in the nation and one that has spawned a number of young recruits for the designated East African terrorist group, Al Shabab.

- In Congress, Rep. Ellison has cultivated extensive, close and ongoing relationships with Sharia-supremacist groups known to be associated with the Muslim Brotherhood. These include notably: the Council on American-Islamic Relations (CAIR), the Islamic Circle of North America (ICNA), the Islamic Society of North America (ISNA) and the North American Islamic Trust (NAIT), among others. His pilgrimage to Mecca required of faithful Muslims, the *hajj*, was paid for by the Brotherhood's overt arm in the United States, the Muslim American Society (MAS).

- Rep. Ellison has continued to associate with these groups and their leadership, appearing and speaking at their conferences even after they were listed by the Department of Justice as unindicted co-conspirators in the 2008 Holy Land Foundation (HLF) Hamas terror-financing trial, the largest in U.S. history.

- Mr. Loudon lists over 500 donors associated with these Sharia-supremacist groups who gave Ellison nearly a quarter of a million dollars over the period from 2006-2017. Among them is the SAAR Network which was investigated by the federal government after 9/11 for its contributions to al-Qaeda and Osama bin Laden.

- Rep. Ellison has also been involved with the U.S. Council of Muslim Organizations (USCMO) from its founding in 2014.

The USCMO is the political umbrella group for the Muslim Brotherhood in America and its fronts—as identified by the Brotherhood's own 1991 Explanatory Memorandum as well as Justice Department evidence in the HLF trial—comprise most of the USCMO's membership.

- Thanks to his regular attendance at and keynote speeches for the USCMO's events, Rep. Ellison has also been associated with the increasingly jihadist regime of Turkish President Recep Tayyip Erdogan, which co-sponsors and is an ever-more-dominant force in that umbrella group's efforts to influence American elections.

Trevor Loudon has done an extraordinary job in researching and compiling this deeply concerning set of facts about Keith Ellison's associations, donors and supporters. It is the kind of work that should be done by a federal background check—not just for him, but for *any* legislators who serve on congressional committees dealing with such sensitive matters as banking and financial services, foreign relations, armed services, homeland security and intelligence. But it is not. And as Mr. Loudon points out, it is unlikely that America's enemies, foreign or domestic, are unaware of this glaring gap in U.S. national security practices.

While Keith Ellison has obvious reasons for wanting you to burn this book, I strongly encourage you instead to read carefully its documentation of the Congressman's unapologetic and ongoing associations with what can only be described as subversive enemies of the state.

Frank J. Gaffney
President and CEO
Center for Security Policy

Chapter One

Who Is Keith Ellison?

There are, or should be, basic expectations for elected officials in general, but particularly related to those serving in the federal government. All members swear an oath to the Constitution of the United States and so adherence to the rule of law is expected and required by vigilant constituents.

Unfortunately, the federal government is a target for subversive elements whose goal is not to uphold the Constitution but rather to gain power for their own ends, and the ends of those they serve. America's founding fathers understood this "nature of government" and carefully embedded checks and balances into the federal government structure. As Thomas Jefferson wrote in 1788, "[T]he natural progress of things is for liberty to yield, and government to gain ground."[1]

These subversive elements, however, are patient and dedicated, oftentimes presenting as patriotic public servants while relentlessly undermining the foundations of America's Constitution.

As this essay will illustrate, Representative Keith Ellison (D-MN) is not a friend of the Constitution and would fail the most cursory security background check required of any low-level federal government employee.

Troubling ties

Rep. Keith Ellison has long-standing and ongoing ties to many individuals and organizations that pose a very real and potential threat to America. He also serves on the House Financial Services Committee and the House Democratic Steering Committee.

Importantly, Rep. Ellison also serves as Vice Chair of the Democratic National Committee.

The House Financial Services Committee has jurisdiction over the banking system, stock exchanges, and the housing and insurance industries. The Committee also handles policy matters including monetary policy, international finance, and combats terrorist financing.

The House Democratic Steering Committee determines the party's platform and committee assignments for Democratic members.

All these positions would make Keith Ellison a prime target for influence operations, or straight out recruitment, by foreign or domestic hostile entities. Would Keith Ellison use his influential position to advance policies beneficial to America's enemies? What is to stop him, other than his presumed loyalty to the United States?

Family background

Keith Ellison was born in Detroit, Michigan in 1963. By all accounts, the future activist and congressman had a happy family life with hard-working and loving parents. His father, Leonard Ellison, Sr., was a psychiatrist, an atheist, and a Republican. Keith's mother Clida is a "devout Catholic from a Louisiana Creole family." Leonard's mantra, according to Ellison, was "There are no handouts or handups."[2]

Ellison's maternal grandfather Frank Martinez, by contrast, was a "voting rights organizer" with the Louisiana NAACP.[3,4] Ellison described "Grandpa Frank" as a "civil rights activist, fighting for civil rights and voting rights" and claimed to have been harassed by the Ku Klux Klan, who allegedly once set a burning cross across the street[5] from their home on Lee Street.

Embracing activism

After graduating from high school in 1981, Keith Ellison majored in economics at nearby Wayne State University.

After joining the student newspaper, the South End, Ellison appears to have had his first taste of notoriety after he "persuaded the editor to publish a cartoon featuring five identical black men dribbling a basketball alongside a man in a Klan robe who was clutching a club."

From Mother Jones:

Above it was a question: "How many Honkies are in this picture?" It was meant to poke fun at racial caricatures, but students didn't see the humor. An African American classmate stormed into the newspaper's office to confront him—a scene Ellison breezily recounted in a follow-up column mocking the outcry. His critics were 'still living in the Jim Crow era,' Ellison wrote. The firestorm made the pages of the Detroit Free Press.

As time went on, Ellison became more and more involved in radical activism. After the widely publicized "Subway Vigilante," Bernard Goetz was acquitted after shooting four alleged black muggers on a New York City subway, Ellison was quoted saying that it will soon be "open season on the brothers."[6]

In his book,[7] Ellison claimed that he "became consumed with understanding racial hierarchy, the economic order, and the structure of society." He joined the Black Student Union. He devoured books by Marxists Frantz Fanon and Saul Alinsky. He was enamored by "crusading attorneys" such as Clarence Darrow, who "defended Socialist Eugene Debs, radical labor leader Big Bill Haywood and assorted anarchists, communists, gangsters and psychopaths"[8] and Communist Party USA front activist William Kunstler, a "radical lawyer" who among other milestones, "had a role in the defense of the suspects in the 1993 bombing of the World Trade Center."[9]

Ellison admired local legal activists, including future Michigan Congressmen George Crockett and John Conyers, both lifelong Communist Party "fellow travelers."[10,11]

"I wanted to be like them," wrote Ellison.[12]

Chapter Two

Conversion to Islam

Like his fellow Muslim Andre Carson[13] in the House of Representatives, Keith Ellison was not born Muslim. Ellison first discovered Islam in 1982 as a sophomore at Wayne State University, after walking into a "makeshift mosque" with sheets on the floor in the Wayne State Student Center.

Eventually, Ellison joined the Muslim Center on Rosa Parks Ave, run by Imam Abdullah Bey El-Amin and Mitchell Shamsud-Din, who "followed the teaching of Warith Deen Mohammed," whose father, Elijah Muhammad, "led the Nation of Islam."[14] While Imam Mohammed left the Nation of Islam to lead his flock into the orthodox teachings of Sunni Islam, he returned for a highly-touted reunion[15] with controversial Nation of Islam leader Louis Farrakhan in 2000.

Imam Mohammed sought to bring mainstream Islam to America and was highly successful in his efforts. He became the first Imam[16] to "deliver the invocation for the United States Senate" in 1992 and "led prayers at both inaugurals of President Bill Clinton."

The Imam's efforts did not go unnoticed in the Middle East, where he "met privately with Arab leaders like President Anwar el-Sadat of Egypt" and received a contribution of $16 million from Sheikh Sultan Ben Mohammad al-Qasmini of the United Arab Emirates to open a mosque and a school.[17]

Ellison explained in his book, "My Country, 'Tis of Thee: My Faith, My Family, Our Future," how he revealed his conversion to Islam to his mother over Thanksgiving dinner, when he refused to try the ham, opting for just turkey.[18]

Nation of Islam

Keith Ellison would go on to work closely with the Nation of Islam (NOI), being one of the "key organizers" of the 1995 Million Man March.

In 1998, Ellison also joined a very Nation of Islam-sounding "community group" called "Sincere and Loyal African American Men" (SALAAM). The group wore green T-shirts and shut down local drug houses.[19] Another such group is the "Men Are Responsible To Cultivate Hope" (MARCH), which was founded to organize for the 1995 Million Man March and continues to meet to this day. Ellison still stops by "occasionally."[20]

It wasn't until his 2006 run for Congress that Ellison was confronted with his long-time association with Louis Farrakhan. "I was hoping it wouldn't come up," he told the Star Tribune, when pressed. In a letter to a Jewish community organization, he conceded that Farrakhan's positions "were and are anti-Semitic, and I should have come to that conclusion earlier than I did." Many question Ellison's sincerity, considering his ongoing appearances with Farrakhan in 2013 and his private meeting with Farrakhan (along with fellow Muslim Rep. Andre Carson) in 2016.[21]

When the "Africana Student Cultural Center" sponsored speeches by Louis Farrakhan and one of his associates, campus Jewish/Black relations nosedived. Ellison, who was by now using the pseudonym "Keith E. Hakim," published a series of op-eds in the student paper, the Minnesota Daily defending Farrakhan. In another column he called for a separate nation for blacks, a long-time communist dream which was also promoted at the Million Man March.

Ellison had attended a campus speech by Louis Farrakhan, the Nation of Islam, as far back as 1985, while still at Wayne State.

Ellison has said that he was never a member of the Nation of Islam and that his working relationship with the organization's "Twin Cities study group" (the national organization's term for its chapters) lasted only 18 months.

Ellison has claimed that he was "an angry young black man" who thought he might have found an ally in the cause of economic and political empowerment, and that he overlooked Farrakhan's most incendiary statements because "when you're African American, there's literally no leader who is not beat up by the press."

In 1995 Ellison, appeared at an organizing rally with former Nation of Islam spokesman Khalid Muhammed at the University of Minnesota. Ellison also acted as local Nation of Islam leader in a march at the office of the US Attorney in Minneapolis protesting the indictment of Qubilah Shabazz for conspiring to murder Louis Farrakhan. Ellison charged the Federal Bureau of Investigation (FBI) with conspiring to murder Farrakhan.[22]

Keith Ellison worked closely with the Nation of Islam in the build-up to the October 1995 Million Man March on Washington, D.C.

Million Man March (1995)

Keith Ellison does not deny his role in planning Louis Farrakhan's Million Man March but claims that the Million Man March is where his pivot from Farrakhan began.

According to Mother Jones writer Tim Murphy:

Minister James Muhammad, who in the 1990s led the Nation of Islam's Twin Cities study group, confirms that Ellison served for several years as the local group's chief of protocol, acting as a liaison between Muhammad and members of the community. He was a "trusted member of our inner circle," says Muhammad, who is no longer active in the Nation of Islam. Ellison regularly attended meetings and sometimes spoke in Muhammad's stead, when the leader was absent.

Interestingly, Murphy received an evasive response from the Ellison camp:

An Ellison spokesman declined to answer questions about the congressman's role in the study group and instead replied in an email, "Right wing and anti-Muslim extremists have been trying to smear Keith and distort his record for more than a decade. He's written extensively about his work on the Million Man March and has a long history of standing up against those who sow division and hatred."

Nation of Islam's Million Man March flyer featuring "Keith X Ellison" as a part of "Men Are Responsible to Cultivate Hope" (MARCH) at the Million Man March Organizing Forum

In his book, Ellison says he was "struck by the smallness of Farrakhan's message compared with the moment."

Months later, however, under the byline Keith X Ellison, Ellison wrote an op-ed in the Twin Cities black weekly *Insight News*, defending Farrakhan against charges of antisemitism. Nearly two years later, he endorsed a statement again defending Farrakhan. When Ellison ran (unsuccessfully) for state representative in 1998, *Insight News* described him as "affiliated" with the Nation of Islam. At community meetings, he would reportedly show up in a bow tie, accompanied by the Fruit of Islam, the Nation of Islam's security wing.

"My ideas about Minister Farrakhan have changed in a number of important ways," Ellison said in 2006.[23]

> *Ellison says he favored Louis Farrakhan's teachings on certain subjects, like black self-sufficiency and personal responsibility. He says his law-school writings and other activities were independent of any outside groups. Ellison says his only interaction with the Nation of Islam was for 18 months during the mid-1990s when he worked with the group to organize Minnesotans to attend the Million Man March. Ellison says he hasn't had any involvement with the group since that time and has never been a member of the organization.*

Spike Moss, an organizer who worked with Ellison on the Million Man March, called his reversal "the ultimate betrayal." Louis Farrakhan even recorded a Facebook video condemning Ellison. "If you denounce me to achieve greatness...wait until the enemy betrays you and then throws you back like a piece of used tissue paper to your people."

Most commentators thought that was the end of the Ellison/Farrakhan relationship, until 2018, when news surfaced of a September 2013 meeting in Manhattan.

According to the Nation of Islam's Final Call, October 2, 2013:[24]

> *While in town for the 68th UN General Assembly, the new Iranian president hosted the Honorable Minister Louis*

Farrakhan, Muslim leaders from different Islamic communities and members of the U.S. Congress at a private meeting.

President Hassan Rouhani was elected in June and held the gathering at the One UN Hotel in Manhattan Sept. 24, 2013 across the street from the UN headquarters.

The meeting with President Hassan Rouhani included other Muslims and congressmen Keith Ellison of Minnesota and Andre Carson of Indiana participated in the dialogue.

After the guests were hosted at a dinner, the Iranian president entered and engaged in a warm discussion with guests, including Democratic congressmen Gregory Meeks of New York and Keith Ellison of Minnesota. Abdul Akbar Muhammad, international representative of the Nation of Islam, and Supreme Capt. Mustapha Farrakhan were part of the Nation of Islam delegation.

It is difficult to imagine that the Iranians would have invited both Farrakhan and Ellison to the same private event, had fences not already been mended.

Or perhaps the Iranians invited both parties to broker a reconciliation between two important allies?

CHAPTER THREE

All In With the Hard Left

K eith Ellison moved to the University of Minnesota Law School in 1988, leaving an ever-lengthening trail of controversy in his wake.

In March 1989, Keith Ellison and Kimberly Washington of the "ad hoc police brutality committee" set up a press conference during a Minneapolis City Council meeting to protest the deaths of two black senior citizens, Lloyd Smalley and Lillian Weiss, who were killed during a police drug raid.[25] Earlier that same month, the Socialist Workers Party's weekly newspaper, *The Militant*, advertised[26] a "Militant Forum" on their calendar titled "Stop Police Brutality from Miami to Minneapolis," featuring the same duo: Ellison and Washington along with Denise McInerney, the "Socialist Workers candidate for mayor of Minneapolis."

In college, especially in Minnesota, Keith Ellison forged ties to Trotskyist and Maoist activists that have endured to this day.

Forward Motion, June 1989

In December 1988, Keith Ellison, then President of the Black American Law Students Association, and two other protestors were arrested for spray-painting over "racist and anti-Semitic" graffiti previously painted on the University of Minnesota campus. The protestors added their own "anti-racist" slogans. Members of the Progressive Student Organization were prominent amongst the approximately 30 protestors.[27]

Activist Jordan Kushner, an associate of Ellison's, organized the Progressive Student Organization contingent, which was the local student affiliate of the Maoist-leaning Freedom Road Socialist Organization (FRSO).[28]

Geoff Hahn of the "Progressive Student Network" conducted an interview in Freedom Road's *Forward Motion* in June 1989 with "student leaders" Keith Ellison and Chris Nisan, on "recent police brutality demonstrations in Minneapolis." Referring to Ellison and Nisan as representative of the "student-led community coalition against police brutality emerging in Minneapolis [which] signals the strengthening of student organizing in a stronger Black movement overall."

Keith Ellison was quoted in the article as blaming "white supremacy" and "capitalism" for hurting people of color:

"The responsible activist has to show young [black] folks out there that white supremacy and capitalism are what's putting them in the position they're in," he said.[29]

Chris Nisan at the time was a candidate for U.S. Congress in Minneapolis' Fifth District for the local Socialist Workers Party, a pro-Cuba Marxist-Leninist organization.[30]

"Battling the Rise in Police Brutality." Forward Motion, June 1989 (*Screenshot*)

Keith Ellison speaking at an October 30, 2015, public forum in Minneapolis on affordable housing with former HUD chief Julian Castro and St. Paul Vice President Yusef Mgeni (*Photo via Turtleroad.org*)

Chris Nisan, August Nimtz, and their comrade Yusef Mgeni are mentioned in the Socialist Workers Party publication *"The Militant"* as speaking at various events sponsored by the SWP.[31,32,33,34]

Yusef Mgeni was listed as a key organizer of the October 1995 Million Man March with Keith Ellison[35] and later became the long time CEO of the "Urban Coalition," which was featured at former President Bill Clinton's "Initiative on Race" website.[36]

Decades later, Yusef Mgeni became the St. Paul, MN, NAACP vice president, where he was featured with his old comrade Keith Ellison in a panel discussion about housing that additionally included then-Housing and Urban Development Secretary Julian Castro.[37]

The 'Embassy Suites Five'

Ellison and Nisan worked closely together in the aftermath of a controversial incident at the Embassy Suites hotel that Ellison referred to in his book as the "Embassy Suites Five."[38]

According to Mother Jones writer Tim Murphy:

> *The hotel was a hangout spot for college students, and on that night two parties were happening on the same floor. One was a kegger hosted by a group of white students. The other was a birthday party attended by African American students. It was a low-key gathering; one woman had brought her toddler. But when police responded to a noise complaint about the kegger, they busted up the birthday instead.*
>
> *Partygoers alleged that the cops had called them "niggers." One student at the party, a Daily reporter named Van Hayden, told me an officer had dangled him over the edge of the sixth-floor railing. He left in handcuffs, with a broken nose and a few bruised ribs.*
>
> *The next day, after the students were released, they joined Ellison at the demonstration against police brutality. A few days later, Ellison led about 75 people in a march to City Hall, where they stormed a City Council meeting, forcing officials to yield the floor to Ellison for a 10-minute speech. By then, Ellison was organizing several protests a week and holding press conferences to pressure Minnesota's attorney general to launch a state investigation into the raid. Ellison demanded "public justice."*
>
> *Ellison envisioned a unified front of young black people, white progressive students, organized labor, and American Indians pushing back against the evils of capitalism and white supremacy. "The more the right attacks, the more we have to respond."*

> *Ellison and Chris Nisan's protests did win a victory, albeit a limited one. Four of the five students arrested at the hotel were acquitted of their misdemeanor charges, and Minneapolis set up an independent, if weak, review board to investigate police brutality claims. In 1990, Ellison helped launch the Coalition for Police Accountability, which organized community meetings and published a quarterly newspaper, Cop Watch.*

In 1999, the Freedom Road Socialist Organization split into two competing groups, both keeping the same name. The Fight Back faction (named after the group's newspaper) was strongest in Illinois and Minnesota. "FightBack!" infiltrated several local activist groups, including the well-known "peace" group Women Against Military Madness (WAMM).

According to the *Committee in Solidarity with the People of Syria* from 2015:[39]

> *For the last three years, the presence of members of the Freedom Road Socialist Organization, a dogmatic Stalinist sect, on WAMM's board and the influence of their ideology has resulted in increased intolerance from the WAMM board towards anyone with a differing viewpoint.*

> *Freedom Road has publicly taken a position in support of the Assad government in Syria. FRSO leader Joe Iosbaker has stated that "the Syrian government ought to be defended". He traveled to Syria in June as part of a delegation to certify Assad's fraudulent re-election in the midst of the bloodiest war on the planet. Iosbaker returned to claim that he had witnessed democratic elections where Assad was "given the mandate by the people of Syria".*

When then-Iranian President Mahmoud Ahmadinejad met in New York, September 21, 2010, with 100 leaders and representatives of anti-war, labor, alternative media, and Iranian and Palestinian solidarity organizations, delegates included Sarah Martin of Freedom Road Socialist Organization/FightBack! and

Margaret Sarfehjooy, a board member of *Women Against Military Madness*.[40]

Representative Ellison was quite happy to work with WAMM, despite (or maybe due to) its increasingly Stalinist/Maoist, pro-Syria/Iran orientation.[41]

On July 9, 2008, more than 100 "peace" activists assembled to hear clergymen and civic leaders critique involvement in the Iraq War.

Starting at noon, a dozen speakers took the podium one-by-one, including Roxanne Abbas (co-chair of Women Against Military Madness), and Isaiah Ellison (son of Rep. Keith Ellison), who read an address penned by his father.

In 2009, Roxanne Abbas, of Women Against Military Madness, helped form the *Minnesota Peace Project*. "'Never a meeting without an action!' Most of us know and live by WAMM's motto, but we don't all have the same preferred mode of action. Some like to hit the streets. Some write letters to the editor. Some plan or attend educational programs. Some lobby their members of Congress. And some do it all."

Several WAMM members are leading the development of a statewide network of peace activists and groups with the working name "the Minnesota Peace Project" to influence foreign policy through their elected officials in the U.S. House and Senate

Abbas reported that "Keith Ellison and Wellstone Action have both offered to conduct a training session on lobbying techniques for group members."[42]

Keith Ellison meets with activists raided by the FBI

On September 24, 2010, the FBI raided the homes of twelve leftist activists across the U.S.A. looking for links to foreign terrorist organizations.

In Minneapolis, five homes were raided as well as the "Anti-War Committee office." Several more activists were arrested in the following days, almost all members of Freedom Road Socialist Organization/FightBack!

They were accused of providing support to two State Department-designated communist terrorist organizations—Colombia's Fuerzas Armadas Revolucionarias de Colombia (FARC) and the Popular Front for the Liberation of Palestine.

On November 5, 2010, Representative Ellison held a meeting with five of the raided activists. "While unclear about what legislative action he could take on their behalf, Ellison conveyed dismay with the raids." The activists encouraged Ellison to circulate a "Dear Colleague" letter to other members of the Progressive Caucus asking for support of an investigation of the FBI actions.

Fight Back! Member Sarah Martin, one of the activists who attended the meeting stated,

> *"It was a reasonably good meeting. He certainly understands the seriousness of this and although political times are pretty horrible right now... he's gonna pursue doing a "dear colleague" letter with the progressive caucus... He kept saying of course, he can't stop this Grand Jury but he's gonna do everything he can. He met with us! This is Congressman Keith Ellison, and he met with us in person and gave us you know, a good time - which is - didn't happen at the Senator's office."*

Fight Back! member Tracy Molm, another of the activists who attended stated,

> *"[We asked Ellison to write] a "dear colleague" letter to Obama directly... He said that he's going to look into a "dear colleague" letter and try to get other progressive people in Congress to sign onto it also."*

Representative Ellison sent a letter to then-U.S. Attorney General Eric Holder, expressing concern over the situation and is continued to "work on options to support his constituents affected."

Fight Back! leader Joe Iosbaker gave kudos[43] to progressive members of congress:

> "It was clear that progressive Representatives of the Congress are very concerned about the FBI investigation. Overall, they were very thankful for our visit and for the information and analysis given to them. The level of awareness about the raids and grand jury was varied, from little to full awareness, but the delegation certainly changed that. After the two days, our presence and purpose definitely created a stir in the halls of Congress. "The fact that we were able to interact with 16 legislative aides or Congress people themselves, during an extremely busy time of restructuring leadership in the Congress, exemplifies the attention this matter is receiving."

The Holder Justice Department seemed little interested in following up the FBI's excellent work, and nothing ever came of the raids.

Keith Ellison was also active in the campaign to heal rifts with another terrorist-sponsoring nation: Cuba.

Keith Ellison and Cuba

A May 03, 2013, a Press Release from the Institute for Policy Studies-affiliated Latin America Working Group's Cuba Team stated:[44]

> Due to your action/emails/phone calls we have 59 signatures from House representatives urging President Obama to support travel to Cuba by granting general licenses for ALL current categories of travel.
>
> By eliminating the laborious license application process, especially for people-to-people groups, that is managed by the Office of Foreign Assets Control (OFAC), the majority of the bureaucratic red tape that holds up licensable travel to Cuba would disappear and actually facilitate what the President wanted to see in 2011, liberalized travel regulations.

Signatories included Representative Ellison, who carried on the campaign to recognize Cuba back home in Minneapolis.

The D.C.-Based "Institute for Policy Studies" is hard-left think tank founded in 1963. The institute follows a "pro-Marxist line on foreign policy, defense and the economy and has spawned a large number of spin-offs, other think tanks and public affairs organizations following the same radical agenda."[45]

From retired lawyer and adjunct law professor, Duane W. Krohnke:[46]

> Minneapolis' Westminster Presbyterian Church has long been connected to Cuba. January 11th, 2015 there was a free concert at the church by Cuban-American jazz pianist Nachito Herrera.
>
> Before the start of the concert itself, Minnesota Congressman Keith Ellison made brief remarks. He said that President Obama's December 17th announcement of the historic changes in the relationship of the two countries demonstrated the importance of persistence and hope for all who have been urging such changes for many years, as had most of the people in the audience. He congratulated us for having this persistence and hope. This lesson also was demonstrated, he said, by the current movie, 'Selma,' which the Congressman recently had seen with his children. His parting injunction to us all: now we all need to keep the pressure on Congress to end the embargo and support the reconciliation.
>
> To a capacity-crowd in our Great Hall, Nachito played Cuban music with great passion. He also told us that he was surprised and overjoyed by the December 17th news of the historic change in the two countries' relationship and wanted to celebrate this important change by sharing his music with Westminster, which he regarded as part of his family.
>
> He also was very happy with the U.S. release from prison of the remaining three members of the Cuban Five, and in recognition of this event he returned his 'Free the Cuban Five' button to two members of the Minnesota Cuba Committee, Prof. August Nimtz, and Frank Curbelo.

Keith Ellison personally knew August Nimtz:

"We oftentimes had these debates and discussions about 'out of the streets and into the suites'—that was the term that was used to describe the swan song of the civil rights movement," says August Nimtz, one of the few black professors at the University of Minnesota and a longtime acquaintance of Ellison's.

August Nimtz, incidentally, was a lifelong member of the Socialist Workers Party, and a comrade of Keith Ellison's '80s activist friend Chris Nisan.[47]

Kwame Ture

In 1990 Ellison participated in the sponsorship of a speech by Kwame Ture (also known as Stokely Carmichael) given at the University of Minnesota Law School entitled "Zionism: Imperialism, White Supremacy or Both?" Keith Ellison rejected the appeal of Jewish law students to withdraw sponsorship of the lecture.[48]

Kwame Ture is credited with popularizing the phrase "black power." He was a leader of the radical Student Nonviolent Coordinating Committee (SNCC), also gained fame as head of the "Prime Minister" of the Maoist leaning Black Panther Party and was additionally a leader of the All-African People's Revolutionary Party.[49]

As reported in his New York Times obituary,[50] during the height of his activism, Ture visited communist countries such as North Vietnam, China, and Cuba. During a speech in Havana, he was quoted as saying:

"We are preparing groups of urban guerrillas for our defense in the cities, he said. It is going to be a fight to the death."

Former Rep. John Conyers, who resigned in 2017 "amid multiplying allegations that he sexually harassed former employees,"[51] told the Communist Party USA publication *The Worker* that he was working with a committee—which included Kwame Ture—to evaluate candidates for the 1968 election, and ultimately to "organize American Negroes into one voting bloc."[52]

Keith Ellison introduces Kwame Ture

Conyers' committee is reminiscent of today's Congressional Black Caucus, of which Keith Ellison is a prominent member.

CHAPTER FOUR

THE LEGAL RIGHTS CENTER

In 1993, after working at the prestigious law firm, Lindquist and Vennum, Ellison became executive director of the Legal Rights Center, a nonprofit focused on "providing indigent defense in the city's African American, Hmong, and American Indian communities."

Center founders included American Indian Movement activist Clyde Bellecourt, a radical leftist and convicted drug dealer.[53]

Sharif Willis and the execution-style murder of Minneapolis police officer Jerry Haaf

Officer Jerry Haaf
(*via MPD Federation*)

On August 16, 1982, Vice Lords gang leader Samuel "Sharif" Willis shot James "Boo" Evans, who came to the defense of his brother Frederick "Cat" Evans, who was arguing with Willis over a $5 gambling dispute. Boo died from a gunshot wound in his back, delivered as he ran across the street away from Willis, who also hit Grover Dickson, aged 71 at the time, with the butt of his rifle as he lay on the ground from being previously beaten. Willis was convicted of murder in the second degree and served six years in prison.[54][55] Willis' prior criminal convictions included "armed robbery and burglary."

27

After serving his time, he started working with young gang members as a prominent member of a "controversial" alternative high school called The City, Inc., which had a program for "at risk youth" which used "older, still-active gang member[s] to bring young gang-bangers in" ostensibly for rehabilitation.[56] Willis also founded a group called "United for Peace," which "pledged to work with authorities to end inter-gang violence."[57]

On September 26, 1992, Minneapolis police officer Jerry Haaf was killed as he was on his coffee break at the Pizza Shack restaurant on East Lake Street in Minneapolis. Haaf was a "30-year veteran of the force and months away from retirement." He had three children.

Vice Lord gang members Shannon Bowles and Mwati (Pepi) McKenzie were ultimately convicted for Officer Haaf's murder, and A.C. Ford Jr., who later changed his name to Adl El-Shabazz and Sharif Willis' 15-year-old nephew Monterey Willis were "convicted on charges that they assisted and planned the killing."

According to testimony, the plot began to gel in Sharif Willis' house where the Vice Lord members were fresh out of a meeting related to an alleged "beating of an elderly blind black man by the Metropolitan Transit Commission (MTC) police." It appears that the meeting incited the young gang members instead of rehabilitating them.

From court documents:[58]

"Witnesses present at the Pizza Shack restaurant on Friday, September 25, 1992, testified that between 1:30 and 2:00 a.m, two or three black males entered the restaurant, walked directly to Officer Haaf, the only uniformed officer in the restaurant, drew revolvers from their belts, and fired at Officer Haaf's back."

While two witnesses "implicated [Sharif] Willis in the planning of the murder," he was never convicted.

As an aside, after the murder, Loverine Harris, the wife of another Vice Lords gang member, Ed Harris, testified that "in the early morning hours on September 25, 1992, Mwati "Pepi" McKenzie and Shannon Bowles arrived at the Harris' apartment and told Ed Harris that they had just shot a man and wanted to change their clothes, hide the guns, and clean up." After police interviewed Ed Harris, his fellow gang members became suspicious and shot and killed him.[59]

Enter Keith Ellison,[60] who jumped into the fray shortly after the brutal murder by "leading events including appearances with [Sharif] Willis and support for Willis's *United for Peace* gang front."

At a rally held in October 1992, Keith Ellison was quoted as saying:

> *"The main point of our rally is to support United for Peace [in its fight against] the campaign of slander the police federation has been waging."*

According to a St. Paul Pioneer Press report cited by Scott Johnson of Powerline Blog, Sharif Willis also spoke at the rally, saying that "Minneapolis police are experiencing the same fear from young black men that blacks have felt from police for many years." Willis said,

> *"We seem to have an overabundance of bad police...we're going to get rid of them. They've got to go."*

The October 11, 1992 edition of Minneapolis' Star Tribune[61] also covered the rally, which was held "one day after a downtown rally in support of police." Author Steve Brandt described an occasion with "often-angry rhetoric." According to the article, Keith Ellison "accused the Police Officers Federation of Minneapolis of trying to appeal to the worst fears of the white community to gain more resources to control minority residents." Mel Reeves, who refers to Minneapolis police as a "a real racist vigilante force"[62] at a publication called "*The Black Activist-Journal of the Black Left Unity Network*" was listed as a "co-chair" of the rally.

Incidentally, Reeves wrote a rambling commentary[63] at the Minneapolis *Spokesman Recorder*, criticizing the Democratic

National Committee for denying Keith Ellison the role as leader, surmising that the DNC feared that "Ellison would write social justice checks that the party wouldn't be willing to cash."

Scott Johnson points out that Ellison also spoke at a demonstration in February 1993 "in support of one of the Haaf murder defendants during the defendant's trial." Ellison reportedly "led the crowd assembled at the courthouse in a chant: 'We don't get no justice, you don't get no peace.'"

In the spring of 1993, Ellison and Willis reportedly attended the "Gang Summit," later renamed "the National Urban Peace & Justice Summit" in Kansas City, where Ellison promoted "police cooperation with gangs to combat crime."

The alliance ended quickly on October 21, 1994, when *United for Peace* founder Sharif Willis "held a dozen people at gunpoint in a north Minneapolis service station, hitting one across the head, ordering them down on the floor, jumping on another, and vowing to 'ice' them all with a Tec-9 semi-automatic pistol." At his side was "an armed 15-year-old gang member." Willis ultimately received a 25-year sentence, which he served.

In 2017, Willis was released and promptly organized a "Peace Summit" with some of the same organizers who attended the rally with Keith Ellison shortly after the murder of Police Officer Haaf.[64]

Ironically, or not, Keith Ellison's ex-wife Kim worked as a math teacher at The City Inc. from 1996–1999.

"A bourgeois pig," "black gangs and white crime hysteria"

Mother of four Myrna Opsahl was at the Crocker National Bank depositing her church's donation plate collections when she was shot and killed by Symbionese Liberation Army (SLA) member Emily Montague Harris. Opsahl's husband Trygve was a surgeon at the hospital where Opsahl died on April 21, 1975.[65] Her injury from a shotgun blast to the abdomen was too severe. He could not save her.

While the SLA is known for kidnapping and radicalizing Patty Hearst, granddaughter of publishing magnate William Randolph

Myrna Opsahl (*Nursing School Graduation Photo*)

Hearst, they were violent Marxist radicals who murdered two people[66] and planted bombs under police cars. Their goal was to "incite a guerrilla war against the U.S. government and destroy what they called the 'capitalist state.'"[67]

In her 1982 book, "Every Secret Thing," Patty Hearst admitted to driving the getaway car that day. After killing Opsahl, Emily Harris was quoted as saying, "Oh, she's dead, but it really doesn't matter. She's a bourgeois pig anyway."[68]

Myrna's son Jon was sitting in his high school classroom when a school nurse came to take him from class and ultimately deliver the news that would change his life and spark a decades-long crusade for justice.[69]

One of the SLA radicals involved in the bank robbery that led to the murder of Myrna Opsahl was Kathleen Soliah, who changed her name to "Sara Jane Olson" and moved to Minnesota where she married a physician and had children. During that same robbery, CNN reported that court documents revealed that Olson "...entered the bank with a firearm and kicked a nonresistant pregnant teller in the stomach. The teller miscarried after the robbery."[70]

After decades living the American dream, Olson was finally charged in 1999 for "plotting to kill police officers by planting nail-packed pipe bombs under two squad cars in August 1975."[71] At the time, she referred to her upcoming trial as "a witch hunt" and asked for donations for her legal expenses, "kicking off a fundraising effort by her defense team and supporters."

One of those supporters was Keith Ellison, who followed former terrorist organization Weather Underground leader Bernadine Dohrn, who keynoted a fundraiser for Sara Olson sponsored by the Minnesota chapter of the radical left, communist-founded National Lawyers Guild, on whose steering committee Ellison had once served.

In his speech (titled "Black Gangs and White Crime Hysteria") archived[72] in its entirety on a now-defunct website supporting Olson, Ellison claimed that the former SLA terrorist was "fighting for freedom in the 60's and 70's" and further claimed that those who sought to prosecute her only wanted to "settle scores."

Ellison said in part:

> "Bernardine [Dohrn] made the point better than anyone so far. This is not about justice. This is not about accountability, this is not about public safety. THIS is about SYMBOLISM. This is about MAKING A POINT. This is about saying to you and to me that we are going to get you if you ever try to stand against what we're about. WE'RE GOING TO GET YOU. And we're going to lock you up and we don't care how long it takes, we're going to get you...And it is the idea that the people who fought for social justice and to elevate humanity in the 60's and 70's were WRONG! They were wrong and we're going to prove it because we're going TO LOCK HER UP. That's what it's about."

Another speaker, Peter Erlinder, was the defense attorney for A.C. Ford in in the murder mentioned above of police officer Jerry Haaf. His speech, also archived,[73] gives an indication of the radical nature of the National Lawyers Guild, and of Keith Ellison.

Here is an excerpt (typos included):

> "As the former president of the National Lawyers Guild, I'm happy to say, the first law student organizer of the National Lawyer's Guild was Bernardine Dohrn and that Stuart Hanlon

[both speaking tonight] and Susan Jordan are both longstanding members of the National Lawyer's Guild. Stuart was responsible for the release of Geronimo jiJaga Pratt, who was a Black Panther leader. Keith Ellison [another speaker tonight] is active in the National Conference of Black Lawyers, which is a sister organization of the National Lawyer's Guild, and has struggled with us for the last 30 years, and we're very proud to work together daily."

Sara Jane Olson pleaded guilty in 2001 to two counts of possessing explosives with intent to murder, and in 2003 to second-degree murder. She received a sentence of 14 years in prison and was released after seven years, in 2009.

CHAPTER FIVE

Rainbow Politics and 'Being on the Inside'

Keith Ellison claims he decided to run for the Minnesota State House "after testifying at a hearing on sentencing reform and seeing no black legislators".[74]

According to Ellison's old Socialist Workers Party comrade Professor August Nimtz:

> *"We oftentimes had these debates and discussions about 'out of the streets and into the suites'—that was the term that was used to describe the swan song of the civil rights movement...He made a decision and thought he could make a difference **by being on the inside**." (emphasis added)*

Ellison won his election to become a state representative from North Minneapolis on his second try in 2002, after losing his first attempt in 1998. In 2006 Ellison entered the race to succeed retiring far left Democratic Representative Martin Sabo.

Ellison "labored to show Jewish progressives he'd turned a page". Incredibly, the well-known Farrakhan follower picked up the endorsement of the *American Jewish World*, the Twin Cities-based newspaper. He also "addressed voters' concerns about Farrakhan at the state's largest synagogue".

From the Mother Jones article:[75]

> *Ellison's years of organizing and legal work formed the basis for a coalition. Fashioning himself as a lefty in the mold of progressive icon Paul Wellstone, Ellison adopted the late senator's spruce-green campaign colors and railed against the "Republican lite" leaders of his party. He ran against the Iraq War and pushed for single-payer health care. Also critical was the mobilization of a new constituency in the Twin*

Cities—Muslim Somali Americans, who had begun settling in the area in the 1990s.

Ellison ran a Rainbow Coalition strategy, modelled on the Jesse Jackson Presidential campaigns of 1984 and 1988. The concept was to inspire the base and ignore the moderate Democrats. The political base would be built by stitching together a cross- cultural, multi-racial "progressive" coalition.

Jesse Jackson even joined Ellison on the campaign trail.[76]

From Mother Jones:

In that first primary, Ellison embraced the old-school tactics he aims to bring to the DNC. He ran no campaign ads; instead, he invested in paid community organizers who started their work early, months before a traditional campaign might lumber to life. Ellison often accompanied his organizers on their rounds. They targeted apartment buildings housing immigrants—Russians, East Africans, Latinos—who had little history of political engagement, and they recruited organizers who came from these communities. "You go to Keith's campaign office and it looks like the United Nations," says Corey Day, the executive director of the state Democratic-Farmer-Labor Party. The Minneapolis City Pages called his coalition "the most diverse crayon box of races and creeds a Minnesota politician has ever mustered."[77]

It proved to be a winning formula. Keith Ellison won a very competitive primary, then went on to win the November election handily. The new iteration of the "Rainbow Coalition" is exactly the strategy now being pushed nationally by today's Democratic Party left wing, under Ellison's leadership.

Communist Party USA connections

Contrary to popular opinion, the Communist Party USA (CPUSA) is still active across America, and additionally maintains a presence in Minnesota.

The Party is still allied to the Communist Party of the Russian Federation (successor to the Communist Party of the Soviet Union) and has strong ties to the Communist Parties of Great Britain, Canada, India, Japan, Peoples Republic of China, Vietnam, Cuba, Iraq and even the Tudeh Party of Iran.

In Minnesota, CPUSA, as in many other states, works inside the Democratic Party (or as it is known locally: "Democratic-Farmer-Labor Party" [DFL]).

CPUSA had its eye on Keith Ellison from at least the moment he first ran for Congress in 2006. In August 2006, an article posted at the Communist Party USA's "People's World" newspaper welcomed Ellison's probable election to Congress, comparing him to the late far-left Minnesota Senator Paul Wellstone, and listing his progressive achievements.[78]

> *"If Keith Ellison is elected in November to represent Minnesota's 5th Congressional District, he will bring to the U.S. House of Representatives a fresh progressive voice in tradition of Paul Wellstone. He will also be the first African American congressman from Minnesota and the first Muslim in the U.S. Congress... Peace and justice activists have been volunteering in increasing numbers in the Ellison campaign to refocus attention on Ellison's program. Ellison calls for immediate withdrawal of U.S. troops from Iraq, a universal, single-payer health care system, protection and extension of civil rights to all, including gays and lesbians, and responsible stewardship of the environment".*

The Party threw practical support behind Ellison's campaign. Minnesota Communist Party leader Erwin Marquit and his wife Doris, and comrades Jim and April Knutson were particularly active.

Erwin Marquit (now deceased) was very open about this in his autobiography "Memoirs of a Lifelong Communist."

Here is an excerpt:[79]

In Minnesota, campaigns for nomination as a candidate in a public election starts with winning support at the precinct caucuses, but Rep. Sabo had announced his retirement after the 7 March precinct caucuses. Therefore, Ellison's initial campaign had to focus on winning the endorsement at the Fifth Congressional District DFL Convention on 6 May from among the convention delegates that had already been chosen at the precinct caucuses. Doris and I normally attend the DFL caucuses. I already have indicated that although the DFL caucus rules state that a participant in the caucus cannot be a member of another political party, the Communist Party is technically not a political party in Minnesota if does not field candidates in the election.

Doris and I had been chosen as delegates for the DFL Congressional District Convention, and we campaigned for Ellison before and at the convention. Ellison, with his strong antiwar position and positive reaction to his role in the legislature as a representative of his predominately African American north Minneapolis district, came out first in the first ballots at the convention, during which Nelson Pallmeyer withdraw and gave his support to Ellison. Ellison won the nomination in the fourth ballot. He still had to face a primary election in September with the four other candidates, all with heavy political credentials that were running against him. To gather support for Ellison, I suggested to April Knutson and Jim Knutson that they draft a letter addressed to activists in the peace movement urging them to support Ellison.

Doris and I and the Knutsons then solicited signatures to the letter from among well-known peace activists. In July, we circulated the letter as widely as possible. Doris and I volunteered to cosponsor a fundraiser for Ellison in our home on 24 July with our neighbors Dave Holets and his wife Nancy Arneson. Dave, already retired, had been in charge of managing the finances of the School of Physics and Astronomy. Together, we leafleted the immediate neighborhood with invitations to the fundraiser. On 21 and 22

> *July, I went into St. Louis Park, a suburb just west of the city line, a block and a half from our home, to do door knocking. When someone appeared at the door, I would begin by introducing myself by name. I was not surprised when one of the first responses I got was, "Oh, you're the Communist at the University of Minnesota." Two or three others recognized me in a similar manner. The fact that I was campaigning for Ellison did not seem to bother any of them.*

Almost immediately after entering Congress in 2007, Ellison riled much of his far-left base by voting to extend funding for the Iraq War. To explain himself Ellison held a community meeting Sunday, April 15, 2007, at the Powderhorn Park Building in South Minneapolis.

From *Pulse Twin Cities* (archived):[80]

> *Ellison admitted that the vote was very hard for him personally. He said he voted for the bill because, for the first time, a congressional bill set an exit date from Iraq. 'It is more different to govern than it is to be in the opposition. A majority of Democrats from 'blue dogs' (Democrats considered to be conservative) to the Out of Iraq caucus came together under the leadership of Speaker Nancy Pelosi to successfully challenge Bush's war without end,' Ellison said. Pelosi had promised the Congressional Progressive Caucus an up-or-down vote later on invading Iran, and Ellison expressed confidence in her leadership.*

Not all were happy with this explanation.

Socialist Alternative member Ty Moore called the Democrats a war party and called on Ellison to break with them--and build an independent movement to bring the war to an end.

One of Ellison's old Maoist friends, lawyer Jordan Kushner said, "Keith's vote showed that his loyalty to the Democratic Party exceeded his loyalty to the peace movement. The peace movement was at the base of his campaign. We thought he was one of us when he pledged not to fund the war." Kushner said that Ellison "could not have won the DFL endorsement and the DFL primary without the active involvement of the peace community."

> *Communist Erwin Marquit came to Ellison's defense, however. He said we needed to take every opportunity to weaken Bush's authority. 'This is just one step in a strategy to bring the war to an end. But we need to keep the pressure on--outside the halls of Congress,' Marquit said. He recalled that, in 1972, the Minnesota Legislature passed a resolution telling the state's attorney general not to send any Minnesota National Guard members to Vietnam. The state Supreme Court later overruled that resolution. 'The important thing is this kind of struggle keeps pressure on and empowers the antiwar movement' Marquit said."*[81]

Erwin Marquit and his wife Doris, also a CPUSA member, hosted *at least three* meetings in their home for Representative Ellison.

From Marquit's memoirs (p. 576):

> *I mentioned earlier that we had three fund raisers, that is, house parties, for Keith Ellison. They were cosponsored again by our friends Nancy Arneson and Dave Holets. The year 2011 was not a Congressional election year. Nevertheless, Ellison's campaign committee needed to raise funds to cover the cost of mobilizing people into activity on the progressive political issues that he supported independently of the actual reelection campaigns. Our third house party, again in our home, was held on 1 September. I asked Marion Greene, who represented our district in the Minnesota House of Representatives to introduce Ellison when it came time for him to speak. About twenty-five people attended. We raised $1,620.*

At one of the Marquit gatherings held on December 17, 2013, Representative Ellison told the assembled comrades about his recent trip to the Middle East:[82]

One question concerned foreign policy: more specifically, a two-state solution the Israel/Palestine issue. Rep. Ellison discussed the current negotiations with Secretary of State John Kerry but said Prime Minister Netanyahu is 'hypocritical' on the settlement issue. He said he took a trip to the region in the summer, visiting many areas not part of the 'official' delegation trips. He spoke of his visit to Hebron, where he said '1,800 Palestinian shops' had been shuttered. He also stressed the need to tap into the Israeli citizenry, who are angry with their government over the occupation

Rep. Ellison even penned an article[83] in the CPUSA's *"People's World"* published on August 29, 2014 discussing the rise of "people's movements" in the United States.

Screenshot from Keith Ellison's article posted at CPUSA publication "People's World"

Ellison wrote in part:

Workers are leading movements for better pay and higher working standards all over the country. Federal contract workers successfully organized last year to urge Democratic President Barack Obama to sign an executive order raising their pay. The Congressional Progressive Caucus, which I co-chair, supports this campaign. We passed amendments earlier this year in Congress to stop federal contractors who steal from their employees from receiving federal contracts.

As a member of the "Political Mobilization Committee" of the Minnesota State AFL-CIO Retirees Council, most of Erwin Marquit's phone-banking consisted of phone calls to union retirees organized by the Minneapolis AFL-CIO Regional Federation. At several of the sessions, almost half of those participating in the phone banking were brought there by the Communist Party USA. The late Doris Marquit also participated in several of these sessions, as well as in those directly organized by the Ellison campaign committee.

CHAPTER SIX

OUT WITH THE COMMUNISTS, IN WITH DEMOCRATIC SOCIALISTS OF AMERICA

Radical Rabbi Michael Lerner and the Democratic Socialists of America

While Keith Ellison's ties to the Minnesota Communist Party appear to have waned since the 2015 death of local leader Erwin Marquit, Ellison's connections to the often-more-militant, and much larger "Democratic Socialists of America" (DSA) have been steadily increasing.

In his book "My Country, Tis of Thee," Keith Ellison claims that his "vision of the politics of generosity and inclusion" came after meeting and talking with California Rabbi Michael Lerner.[84]

A Progressive Rabbi, and early Democratic Socialists of America member,[85] Michael Lerner was also a "9/11 Truther"[86] and a former supporter of the 1970s pro-Cuban terrorist organization, the Weather Underground.

In the period after the formation of the Weathermen at Flint Michigan, Michael Lerner and Weathermen Chip Marshall, Jeff Alan Dowd and Joseph H. Kelly moved to Seattle to form the "Seattle Liberation Front" to "bring the revolution to Seattle." Several members of this group were later indicted for a February 17, 1970 attack on a Federal building.[87]

As an aside, Ellison's "generous and inclusive" comrade Michael Lerner "was soliciting funds to bring Stokely Carmichael [Kwame Ture] to Berkeley" in 1966, whom Ellison would end up sponsoring 24 years later, as described previously.

Keith Ellison was given support in his 2006 and 2010 Congressional races by a group euphemistically called the "21st Century Democrats," a Political Action Committee (PAC), which was chaired by former St. Paul Minnesota mayor Jim Scheibel, a longtime member of Democratic Socialists of America[88] On August 13, 2006, Jim Scheibel and fellow DSA comrade Minnesota state representative Michael Paymar hosted a fundraiser for Keith Ellison in a private home in St Paul.[89]

In 2009 Keith Ellison was listed as a member of the Advisory Board of Wellstone Action, a Minnesota based organization based on the political legacy of that state's late 'progressive" Senator Paul Wellstone. Also serving on the Advisory Board were DSA members Deborah Olson, Julian Bond and Frances Fox Piven.[90]

The young Keith Ellison had been a Wellstone "disciple". [91] Senator Wellstone himself had been a longtime Democratic Socialists of America supporter, and in turn received assistance from the DSA for his various reelection needs.[92]

In 2011, Keith Ellison was honored with a "Progressive Leadership Award" by the DSA-controlled "Midwest Academy," a Chicago school based on the teachings of radical "community organizer" Saul Alinsky.[93]

In 2013, Rep. Keith Ellison served on the Board of Directors of the D.C.-based Economic Policy, an organization lead by long time DSA comrade Larry Mishel of The New School for Social Research. Ellison served alongside DSA supporters Jeff Faux, Robert Kuttner of The American Prospect, Leo Gerard of the United Steelworkers, DSA member Teresa Ghilarducci, Pedro Noguera from the University of California Los Angeles (and once a supporter of the pro-China "League of Revolutionary Struggle," and Tom Perez of the Democratic National Committee.[94]

Ironically Democratic Socialists of America would back Ellison (unsuccessfully) against Tom Perez in the 2016 battle for the Democratic national Committee chairmanship.[95]

This is the Statement of the National Political Committee of Democratic Socialists of America, February 27, 2016:

> *This weekend the Democratic National Committee (DNC) failed to choose Representative Keith Ellison (D-MN) for Chair of the DNC. Democratic Socialists of America (DSA) backed Ellison's election as part of a rebellion of progressive*

Democratic Party activists against a neoliberal Democratic Party national leadership that places corporate interests ahead of the interests of working people...

DSA understood that the Democratic Party establishment would use every tactic to oppose Ellison, including a whisper campaign that the party could not afford to have a Muslim as its party chair.

DSA viewed the Ellison campaign as just one small part of a broader struggle to develop a majoritarian politics—both at the ballot box and in the streets—that defends the interests of working people of all races, genders and nationalities against the super-rich and corporations...

DSA worked with a broad coalition of trade unions, [Bernie] Sanders campaign veterans, and Black, Latino, Asian-American and indigenous activists to elect Ellison chair of the DNC. The close nature of the race shows the growing strength of these social forces...

DSA remains committed to broadening out the post-Sanders trend into a multiracial majoritarian coalition for the democratic socialist alternative to both neoliberal capitalism and right-wing nationalism. The need for a political revolution is as pressing as ever.

Progressive Democrats of America connection

> "...many members of DSA have joined PDA and taken part in its campaigns... We have welcomed and supported PDA's project of petitioning Bernie Sanders to run for president. We in DSA are committed to help PDA..."[96]

—Maria Svart, National Director, Democratic Socialists of America, May 2, 2014

After the Ellison Defeat: Continuing the Struggle Against the Neoliberal Democratic Party Establishment

Statement of the National Political Committee of Democratic Socialists of America
February 27, 2016

This weekend the Democratic National Committee (DNC) failed to choose Representative Keith Ellison (D-MN) for Chair of the DNC. Democratic Socialists of America (DSA) backed Ellison's election as part of a rebellion of progressive Democratic Party activists against a neoliberal Democratic Party national leadership that places corporate interests ahead of the interests of working people.

Official statements from the DSA's National Political Committee. "After the Ellison Defeat: Continuing the Struggle Against the Neoliberal Democratic Party Establishment," February 27, 2017 (*Screenshot*)

Representative Keith Ellison also has close ties to the Progressive Democrats of America (PDA), having joined their Advisory Board in 2013. PDA is effectively a front for Democratic Socialists of America and the Institute for Policy Studies.

An article by PDA Executive Director Tim Carpenter[97] in DSA's *Democratic Left Magazine*'s Fall 2006 issue (official publication of Democratic Socialists of America) profiled the organization:

> *Progressive Democrats of America is a rapidly growing, two-year-old, 80,000-strong, 135-chapter organization operating in over 30 states. PDA's board of advisers is a diverse group of committed progressive elected officials and activists.*
>
> *Since its founding in Roxbury, Massachusetts, in July 2004, PDA has aggressively worked an "inside/outside" strategy, networking progressive Democratic elected officials inside the Beltway with grassroots Democrats and progressive movement activists across the country.*

Longtime Democratic Socialists of America member Tim Carpenter[98] claimed that Progressive Democrats of America had chalked up several achievements in its short life, successfully promoting initiatives by PDA board members John Conyers and James McGovern.

> *PDA was the driving force in the passage of resolutions opposing the war in Iraq by eight state Democratic Party meetings. The organization also was instrumental in the passage of resolutions in 10 states calling for the impeachment of President Bush.*
>
> *PDA is often referred to by Congressional Progressive Caucus Executive Director Bill Goold as the CPC's field operation, because PDA has built relationships with members of Congress by delivering grassroots support for their initiatives—from Rep. John Conyers' investigation of the 2004 Ohio voting fraud to Rep. Jim McGovern's bill to cut off funding for the war in Iraq, a current priority effort.*

The now-archived "Inside-Outside Strategy" for the PDA[99] was to build "coalitions outside the Democratic Party on shared issues." Furthermore, the goal was to aggressively organize so that chapters were "established" in "all 435 congressional districts."

Other board members have included far left activists Medea Benjamin, Tom Hayden and Cindy Sheehan, who served alongside elected representatives such as John Conyers, Kyrsten Sinema and Maxine Waters, to name a few.[100]

In 2012, PDA "hit its stride electorally" as well helping its National Board Members Congress members John Conyers (D-MI.), Donna Edwards (D-MD.), Keith Ellison (D-MN.), Raul Grijalva (D-AZ.), James McGovern (D-MA.) and Barbara Lee (D-CA.) sweep to victory.[101]

Progressive Democrats of America has endorsed Keith Ellison, a regular at PDA events and Capitol Hill "roundtables," every election cycle since 2012.

As of May 2018, Ellison serves on the PDA Advisory Board alongside Michael Lighty of DSA and DSA-led labor union "National Nurses United," Bill Fletcher, Jr. of the "Institute for Policy Studies" and "Freedom Road Socialist Organization" and Marjorie Cohn, assistant deputy secretary general of the Cold War era Soviet front "International Association of Democratic Lawyers."[102]

For several years PDA and "National Nurses United" have promoted the so-called "Robin Hood Tax". Originating out of the European socialist movement, the Robin Hood Tax would levy a 1% tax on *all* financial transactions.

Representative Ellison followed through by introducing a bill in Congress:

> *April 7, 2014, (Metropolitan Washington Council, AFL-CIO) DCNA's Sandy Falwell joined Rev. Rodney Sadler, Rep. Keith Ellison, and Amanda Lugg and other activists at the U.S. Capitol last Friday to connect Dr. Martin Luther King, Jr.'s fight for economic justice with a tax on Wall Street to fund efforts to reverse inequality.*
>
> *"The Inclusive Prosperity Act would make Dr. King proud," said Rep. Keith Ellison at a kick off press conference in Washington against the backdrop of the U.S. Capitol. ...*

And on this day in 2014 Rep. Ellison spoke of the Robin Hood Tax, embodied in his bill, H.R. 1579, a sales tax on Wall Street speculative trading that would create hundreds of billions of dollars a year in revenue for communities in need, a way to attain the economic equality Dr. King was seeking.

When PDA director Tim Carpenter died in April 2014, Keith Ellison wrote a tribute to him, stating in part that Carpenter "showed the kind of determination and courage that was contagious. His passionate idealism was matched only by his inexhaustible commitment to making those dreams a reality."[103]

Tim Carpenter (left) and Keith Ellison

Congressional Progressive Caucus

Progressive Democrats of America is effectively the electoral wing of the Congressional Progressive Caucus, the most overtly leftist grouping in the House of Representatives. It serves a transmission belt, for hard left socialist policies, into the broader Democratic Party. Under the Grijalva/Ellison leadership, it was unquestionably the most powerful wing of the Party.

Keith Ellison joined the Congressional Progressive Caucus (CPC) soon after taking his seat in 2007 and has remained a member ever since. Ellison has served several leadership roles in the Caucus from 2012 until he was elected vice chair of the Democratic National Committee in 2016. He has served as Progressive Caucus co-chair with Arizona Rep. Raul Grijalva.

The CPC was founded in 1991 by then-freshman Congressman Bernie Sanders. Sanders' CPC co-founders included House members Ron Dellums, Lane Evans, Tom Andrews, Peter DeFazio, and Maxine Waters. As an aside, Ron Dellums, despite serving on the House Armed Services Committee, was a card-carrying member of Democratic Socialists of America.[104],[105]

Except for Tom Andrews, all the others were endorsed or supported by DSA in various Congressional races.

According to Chicago DSA, Democratic Socialists of America played a role in organizing the Congressional Progressive Caucus:[106]

> *Congressman Bernie Sanders has been charging that these bail-outs to regimes which violate worker and civil rights are illegal under a law passed last year by Sanders and Representative Barney Frank, both leaders of the Progressive Caucus in Congress which DSA has helped to organize...*

Ron Dellums (right), Chicago Democratic Socialists of America, 1983

In 1999 the Young Democratic Socialists of James Madison University wrote:[107]

> D.S.A. is not a political party, but rather works within the left wing of the Democratic Party and other third parties. D.S.A. is a driving force for the Progressive Caucus in the U.S. House of Representatives (led by Rep. Bernie Sanders, Socialist Congressman of Vermont).

According to a DSA flier, the organization works with the Congressional Progressive Caucus to promote "*progressive change.*"[108]

> DSA is an activist organization, not a political party. From promoting single-payer health care, to combating Congress' war on the poor, to proposing democratic alternatives to the power of the transnational corporations, DSA is in the center of struggles to advance a progressive America. This struggle is carried on not only by prominent leaders, but more importantly, through the work of thousands of DSA members across the country.

> Since 1982, DSA has been working for progressive change. As a national organization, DSA joins with its allies in Congress' Progressive Caucus and in many other progressive organizations, fighting for the interests of the average citizen both in legislative struggles and in other campaigns to educate the public on progressive issues and to secure progressive access to the media.

> As activists in DSA locals and student chapters from Boston to San Diego, our members take part in local and state campaigns for economic, political, and social justice, while also supporting DSA's national efforts.

The Communist Party USA also has ties to the Congressional Progressive Caucus.

A 2002 report by Joelle Fishman, Chair, Political Action Committee, Communist Party USA to the Party's National Board, evaluated the Congressional Progressive Caucus:[109]

> *Although this Caucus is not large enough to control the Congressional agenda or even to break into the media, the existence of this group of 57 members of Congress, which includes 20 members of the Congressional Black Caucus and six members of the Congressional Hispanic Caucus, provides an important lever that can be used to advance workers' issues and move the debate to the left in every Congressional District in the country.*

A report praising Barack Obama, and the changes wrought by him, as well as communist connection to the Democratic Party, was delivered at the 14th International Meeting of Communist and Workers Parties, held in Beirut, Lebanon, November 22-25, 2012, by Keith Ellison's old comrade Erwin Marquit, then a member of the International Department, CPUSA:[110]

> *In our electoral policy, we seek to cooperate and strengthen our relationship with the more progressive elements in Democratic Party, such as the Progressive Caucus in the U.S. Congress, a group of seventy-six members of the Congress co-chaired by Raúl Grijalva, a Latino from Arizona, and Keith Ellison, an African American Muslim from Minnesota. We also will strengthen our relationship to the Congressional Black Caucus (formed by African Americans in the Congress), which has been the point of origin of innovative policies including an end to the U.S. economic blockade of Cuba...*

> *In its domestic policy, for example, the Progressive Caucus has put forth a program for using the public sector to deal with unemployment. It has opposed the use of the so called "war on terror" to incarcerate U.S. citizens indefinitely without criminal charges. In its foreign policy, the Progressive Caucus and the Black Caucus are outspoken in their opposition to U.S. imperialist policies abroad.*

> *The Progressive Caucus, now that Obama has been reelected, will be playing an important role in contributing to the mobilization of mass activity on critical issues to bring pressure on the Congress and administration to act on them...*

The Congressional Progressive Caucus is simply a transmission belt for socialist policies into the US Congress.

"Responding directly to national demand for a massive jobs program," members of the Congressional Progressive Caucus, December 13, 2011, introduced the "Restore the American Dream for the 99 Percent Act" into the House of Representatives.

> *The bill would create more than 4 million jobs and reduce the deficit by more than $2 trillion over the next 10 years, making it the biggest government effort thus far to marshal the resources needed to address the economic crisis.*
>
> *While no one expects the bill to pass in the Republican-controlled House, it is viewed by many as outlining what really must be done if the economy is to be restarted in a way that benefits the overwhelming majority of the population.*

Progressive Caucus Co-Chairmen Reps. Keith Ellison, D-Minn. and Raul Grijalva, D-Ariz., presented the legislation at a news conference in the Capitol.[111]

> *The bill would create several "corps" that will offer government jobs to the unemployed doing essential work including repairing school buildings, maintaining public parks, building neighborhood energy efficiency and conservation projects, and providing health care and other public services in underserved areas...*
>
> *The bill includes provisions that would raise $800 billion through a surcharge on millionaires and billionaires, end tax subsidies for oil companies, and impose a tiny financial transactions tax on Wall Street.*
>
> *There would be other budget savings through ending the war in Afghanistan and slashing $200 billion from the defense*

budget by eliminating unneeded weapons systems and cutting in half the military forces currently stationed in Europe.

The bill also strengthens health care reform by creating a public health insurance option that would be available through health care exchanges. That measure alone, the lawmakers say, would drive down spending federal health care spending by $90 billion.

"This bill," said Ellison, "shows we can put people to work today by building for tomorrow."

Congressional Black Caucus

Representative Ellison has long been, and remains, a rank and file member of the Congressional Black Caucus (CBC).

Founded in 1971 by far-left Congress members such as Shirley Chisholm, John Conyers, Ron Dellums, Augustus Hawkins, Parren Mitchell, and Charles B. Rangel, the CBC was a conduit for policies designed to destroy Apartheid South Africa, and to assist communist Cuba.

Writing in the Cuba Communist Party journal *Granma*, Fidel Castro gave a history of the CBC and its relations with Cuba in his 2009 article, "[T]he seven Congress members who are visiting us":[112]

An important US political delegation is visiting us right now. Its members belong to the Congressional Black Caucus (CBC) which, in practice, has functioned as the most progressive wing of the Democratic Party.

The Congressional Black Caucus was founded in January 1969 by the 12 African-American legislators who were members of the U.S. Congress at that moment.

Presently, as a result of the struggles they have waged, the CBC has 42 members. Several of its representatives have maintained very active and constructive positions on Cuba-related topics.

The late academic/activist Manning Marable, a fellow traveler of the pro-China Communist Workers Party and a leader of both Democratic Socialists of America and the Committees of Correspondence for Democracy and Socialism, wrote in 2003:[113]

> *That the Congressional Black Caucus is the most progressive organized formation in national politics is not an accident. The CBC's politics are what they are because of the base they reflect. To the degree this base socially fragments and deteriorates and becomes splintered from the broad progressive movement is the degree to which the entire progressive movement is weakened.*

CHAPTER SEVEN

BACK IN THE FOLD OF ORTHODOX SUNNI ISLAM

Mecca and the Asad Zaman connection

It is uncertain when Keith Ellison returned to orthodox Sunni Islam, but he was clearly back in the fold by the mid-2000s.[114,115]

Key supporters in the 2006 Keith Ellison Congressional campaign included Dan McGrath of "Take Action" Minnesota, Pam Costain (an attendee of the Weather Underground and Prairie Fire Organizing Committee organized Hard Times Conference in January 1976 at the University of Chicago), Dick Kaspari from the National Lawyers Guild, Vic Rosenthal and Frank Hornstein from the Jewish community, and Imam Asad Zaman from the Muslim community.

A Minnesotan since 1992, Zaman, in 2005, co-founded the Muslim Day at the Capitol, a "model of civic engagement and advocacy that has been replicated in several other states". Asad is active in interfaith activities and has trained a Speakers Bureau to deliver presentations at churches, synagogues, corporate, and government offices.

In 2005, he was appointed by the Governor to the Minnesota Board of Teaching. Upon confirmation by the Minnesota senate, he served on it until 2009.

In 2011, he co-founded the Minnesota Rabbi Imam Round Table. He has provided training to over 200 police officers serving in various Minnesota police departments.

Asad Zaman is now Executive Director at Muslim American Society of Minnesota. He has chaired the MAS Minnesota convention several times.[116] The MAS is the self-declared overt arm of the Muslim Brotherhood in the United States.

Ellison and the U.S. Muslim Brotherhood

Before United States Council of Muslim Organizations (USCMO) Secretary General Oussama Jammal invited U.S. Representative Keith Ellison (D-MN) to the USCMO's historic inaugural event in June 2014 in the Washington, DC area, he likely would have been aware that this member of Congress had long maintained a close working relationship with a list representative of most of the top Muslim Brotherhood front groups in the country. Ellison also previously had been a featured speaker at many Muslim Brotherhood-affiliated organizations' events.

A list of some of these Brotherhood events may be found in Appendix A.

Moreover, over a period spanning about eleven years (2006-2017), Ellison took in nearly a quarter of a million dollars in campaign donations (as documented in online reporting)[117] from individuals whose listed affiliation was with an identifiable Muslim Brotherhood front organization. Specifically, from 26 April 2006 through 27 November 2017, Keith Ellison received a total of $220,043,[118] which came from a number of organizations closely affiliated with the Muslim Brotherhood, including: American Muslims for Palestine (AMP), Council on American-Islamic Relations (CAIR), Islamic Circle of North America (ICNA), International Institute of Islamic Thought (IIIT), Islamic Society of North America (ISNA), Muslim American Society (MAS), Muslim Public Affairs Council (MPAC), and the North American Islamic Trust (NAIT).

Appendix B displays a list of well over 500 donors to Rep. Keith Ellison for the period 2006-2017 by individuals and groups such as these that are openly identified as affiliated with known Muslim Brotherhood front groups.[119]

Especially troubling is the fact that Congressman Ellison continued taking financial donations from these entities well after the United States Department of Justice listed them as unindicted co-conspirators in the 2008 Holy Land Foundation (HLF) HAMAS terror funding trial.

AMP, CAIR, ICNA, IIIT, and MAS are members of the United States Council of Muslim Organizations (USCMO), which forms the leading edge of the jihadist movement in this country. Clearly, while the USCMO seeks to cloak itself in red, white, and blue, it does so in furtherance of what can aptly be described as "Star Spangled Shariah,"[120] the subversive effort to insinuate Islamic Law (shariah) into U.S. society. Ellison's relationship with the USCMO, beginning as a keynote speaker for the USCMO's inaugural banquet in June 2014, continues seamlessly from his earlier collaboration with the USCMO's Brotherhood member groups.

According to online documentation, Ellison's financial donors by name and their affiliated organizations[121] include the following: Nihad Awad (Executive Director, CAIR); Corey Saylor (Managing Director, Security and Rights at ReThink Media who worked previously for CAIR National); Taher Herzallah (Associate Director of Outreach & Community Organizing for AMP); Esam Omeish (Treasurer, Together We Serve, a USCMO member); Rizwan Jaka (board member, All Dulles Area Muslim Society (ADAMS) Center & ISNA), Yaqub Mirza (board member, IIIT; member of SAAR/SAFA Group, the organization named after its founder, Sulaiman Abdul Aziz Al Rajhi, a senior Saudi close to the royal family and part of what was called the Golden Chain, a list of pre-9/11 al-Qaeda supporters); and Jamal Barzinji (connections to IIIT, ISNA, MSA, NAIT, and SAAR/SAFA).

Jamal Barzinji (deceased, September 2015) and Yaqub Mirza, both financial donors to Rep. Keith Ellison, are IIIT board members. Jamal Barzinji and Yaqub Mirza are listed in declassified U.S. government documents as among[122] "members and leaders of the IKHWAN [or the Muslim Brotherhood]." A source whose name is redacted in the investigative file, according to an FBI memo[123], "advised that the IIIT, NAIT (North American Islamic Trust) and all the subsidiary and sponsoring Muslim organizations under the control of the IIIT and the SAAR Foundation are in fact IKHWAN organizations."[124]

According to the Investigative Project on Terrorism[125], the SAAR Network, also known as the SAFA Group, is a network comprised of up to 100 nonprofit and for-profit organizations that are interrelated through corporate officers and holding companies which have facilitated the funding of jihadist operations. The same address in Herndon, Virginia is shared by many of these organizations.

Federal investigators alleged that the SAAR Network provided support for al-Qa'eda, HAMAS, and the Palestinian Islamic Jihad. The investigation of this network in Operation Green Quest, which raided SAAR's Virginia offices in March 2002, uncovered extensive evidence of material support to jihadists. U.S. Custom Service Agent David Kane, in an application for a search warrant, referenced evidence of the SAAR network's jihadist activity dating back to the 1980s.[126]

For reasons unknown, after some seventy indictments and seized funds amounting to over $30 million by 2003, Operation Green Quest was disbanded in May 2003 under a dubious agreement between the Department of Homeland Security and the Department of Justice.

On the *Hajj*, courtesy of the U.S. Muslim Brotherhood

In December 2008, U.S. Representative Ellison made history as the first member of Congress to make a Muslim American Society (MAS)-sponsored *hajj* pilgrimage to Mecca. MAS was created by the Muslim Brotherhood[127] and is also is a founding member of the USCMO. In 2007 and 2008, Ellison gave the keynote address at MAS conventions in Minnesota.[128] This very same MAS Minnesota chapter that paid for Ellison's *hajj* highlighted writings on its website from Islamic clerics who praised HAMAS and urged Muslims to "wage Jihad until death."[129] The founders of HAMAS and some of Al-Qaeda's founding figures were members of the Muslim Brotherhood first.

In December 2008, as Keith Ellison made his *hajj* pilgrimage to Mecca, he first travelled to Medina where he stayed for several days, meeting up with his friend Asad Zaman and other pilgrims from Minnesota.[130]

After Mecca, Ellison was invited to a reception at the King's residence, for 60 to 70 people from Indonesia, Iran, Pakistan, Palestine, China and Chad. Ellison chatted with a member of the Iranian parliament.

Nearly eight months later, Representative Ellison faced a House Ethics Committee review of his decision to keep the trip's costs secret "even though it was paid for by a local Islamic nonprofit and could have legally been reported as a gift to a public official."

Asked about the trip, Ellison said that he is "not privy to the internal workings of the organization" that covered his costs, and that he complied with all House Ethics panel disclosure requirements. "Why should I waive a right that's accorded me under the rules?" he said.

According to the Star-Tribune:[131]

> *Tax records show the group that paid Ellison's expenses, the Muslim American Society of Minnesota, received nearly $900,000 in taxpayer money in 2006 and 2007 from a rental arrangement for Tarek ibn Ziyad Academy (TiZA), an Inver Grove Heights charter school.*
>
> *Asad Zaman was executive director of the TiZA school, a political contributor of Ellison's and was president of the Muslim American Society until August, when the Mecca trip was planned.*
>
> *TiZA has been sued by the American Civil Liberties Union and probed by state officials for allegedly promoting Islam, which would violate the church and state separation required of public schools -- including charter schools.*
>
> *The school received state funding to pay rent to the Muslim American Society Property Holding Corp., a nonprofit spinoff of the Muslim American Society that owned the building. The corporation then turned over $879,000 to the Muslim society as a grant.*

These connections opened Ellison to ethical questions about the trip. Ellison called it "a private trip," adding that he had told the ethics committee of the trip beforehand and received its approval.

> *A spokesman for the school says no public money was used for the trip, or hajj, which Ellison took as a once-in-a-lifetime fulfillment of his religious duty as a practicing Muslim. The 16-day pilgrimage is considered one of the most solemn acts in Islam, one that is supposed to be undertaken free of debts and unmet family obligations.*
>
> *Ellison has justified withholding the cost by citing the religious nature of his journey to Saudi Arabia, saying it had nothing to do with his duties as a congressman.*

Asad Zaman's Muslim American Society (MAS) is based in Virginia. It was founded by members of the jihadist Muslim Brotherhood in 1993 to act as the "overt arm of the Muslim Brotherhood in the United States," according to Federal prosecutors in 2008 Holy Land Foundation trial.[132]

In December 2017, Imam Zaman shared breakfast with Mr. Mehmet Mehdi Eker, Turkish Member of Parliament and Chair of the foreign relations committee of President Erdogan's Islamic Justice and Development Party (AKP), at the MAS-ICNA Convention in Chicago.[133] Given Turkey's growing role as a world leader of the Islamic Movement, such a meeting is akin to meeting with the Soviet Foreign Minister in 1978.

While in Mecca, Keith Ellison also met America's then-second highest ranking Muslim elected official, North Carolina State Senator Larry Shaw.[134]

The following year, Shaw would become board chairman of America's most vocal Muslim Brotherhood/HAMAS front organization, the Council on American–Islamic Relations (CAIR).[135]

Keith Ellison and CAIR

As may be gleaned readily from the published list of his Muslim Brotherhood-affiliated donors (noted above and in

Appendix B), Representative Keith Ellison and the Council on American–Islamic Relations (CAIR) have a long-standing and particularly close relationship. CAIR claims to be America's largest Muslim civil liberties organization but was founded in 1994 by three of the top U.S. representatives of HAMAS, one of whom (Nihad Awad) continues to serve as its National Executive Director.[136] It has regional offices nationwide, guided by a national headquarters on Capitol Hill in Washington D.C.

> *Since its establishment in 1994, CAIR has worked to promote a positive image of Islam and Muslims in America. Through media relations, government relations, education and advocacy, CAIR puts forth an Islamic perspective to ensure the Muslim voice is represented. In offering this perspective, CAIR seeks to empower the American Muslim community and encourage their participation in political and social activism.*[137]

While CAIR professes to represent American Muslims, the organization in fact serves as a front group for the Palestinian terrorist group HAMAS, and its parent group the Muslim Brotherhood.

Evidence linking CAIR and its founders to a HAMAS-support network has been released through court action, prompting the FBI to cut off its outreach with the group. In 2010, the DOJ said it had seen no "new evidence that exonerates CAIR from the allegations that it provides financial support to designated terrorist organizations."[138]

According to the Investigative Project on Terrorism:[139]

> *CAIR was listed among organizations belonging to an umbrella group of HAMAS-support entities in the United States called the Palestine Committee. In addition, CAIR founders Nihad Awad and Omar Ahmed were included alongside senior Hamas officials such as Mousa Abu Marzook and Ahmed Yousef on a telephone list of individual Palestine Committee members.*

> *That evidence was released in the terror-financing trial of the Holy Land Foundation for Relief and Development (HLF) in Dallas.*

Current CAIR Executive Director Nihad Awad admitted during a March 1994 panel at Barry University that he had been a leader of the General Union of Palestinian Student (the Palestine Liberation Organization's main international support network) but had switched his support to HAMAS.

His exact quote:[140]

> *I used to support the PLO [Palestine Liberation Organization], and I used to be the President of the General Union of Palestine Students which is part of the PLO here in the United States, but after I researched the situation inside Palestine and outside, I am in support of the Hamas movement more than the PLO.*

The General Union of Palestinian Students has long been a member of the still-existing international Soviet front group, the World Federation of Democratic Youth.[141]

It would not be a stretch to consider that Nihad Awad's change of allegiance should coincide closely with the "collapse" of communism. The old Soviet funding networks dried up for a time. The Palestinian Authorities (including HAMAS) were flush with US taxpayer money. Why not take capitalist money to advance the Caliphate/revolution?

CAIR has not forgotten its communist roots. It still works closely with the pro-Russia/ China/ Cuba/ Iran/ North Korea Workers World Party,[142] Party for Socialism and Liberation[143],[144] and Freedom Road Socialist Organization—FightBack,[145] and with the country's largest Marxist organization Democratic Socialists of America.[146]

Keith Ellison has attended many CAIR events. Here are a few of them:

November 2006: More than 1,000 people turned out at the CAIR fundraiser banquet in Arlington, Virginia to hear addresses by several elected officials, including Keith Ellison. The event "raised more than $620,000" for CAIR.

Elected officials who spoke at the sold-out event included Representative-elect Ellison (D-MN), as well as far left Reps. Mike Honda (D-CA), Sheila Jackson Lee (D-TX), and Elijah Cummings (D-MD). Ellison and Jackson Lee offered their addresses by video. Saqib Ali of the Maryland House of Delegates (District 39) was also in attendance.

Other speakers included then-Special Agent in Charge Joseph Persichini, Jr. of the FBI's Washington Field Office, former Fairfax County Police Chief Col. David M. Rohrer, and Amy Goodman of the hard-left media group "Democracy Now."[147]

June 2011: CAIR-LA hosted a community event in San Fernando Valley featuring the first Muslim U.S. Congressman Keith Ellison, who gave a keynote address on the theme, "Defending our Democracy."[148]

> *Congressman Ellison shed light on the current anti-Muslim sentiment in society and how Muslims can effectively challenge it through education and activism.*
>
> *CAIR-LA Executive Director Hussam Ayloush expanded on the organization's key grassroots efforts and community empowerment programs, such as engagement with the Japanese American community to organize Southland Muslims' annual visit to Manzanar internment camp and the resulting high school learning exchange program that brings together Muslim and Japanese American youth.*

Hussam Ayloush had served on the advisory board of the website Electronic Intifada, alongside two former supporters of the pro-China Communist Workers Party.[149]

April 2013: Some 400 people turned out for the 6th Annual Banquet of the Minnesota chapter of CAIR.[150] Senator Amy Klobuchar (D-MN) and Congressman Keith Ellison were special guest speakers. Iowa state Representative Ako Abdul-Samad was the keynote speaker for the event.

CAIR-MN's annual "Justice Works" award was presented to attorney Jordan Kushner, Keith Ellison's old Progressive Student Organization comrade from his University of Minnesota days.

July 2016: CAIR - Philadelphia, American Friends Service Committee and Jewish Voice for Peace hosted a town hall meeting on "Countering Islamophobia."[151]

Speakers at the town hall meeting included Representative Keith Ellison, CAIR National Executive Director Nihad Awad, Linda Sarsour, executive director of the Arab American Association of New York, Kameelah M. Rashad, Muslim chaplain at UPENN, Raed Jarrar, government relations manager at American Friends Service Committee (AFSC), Donna Nevel of the Network Against Islamophobia, Jewish Voice for Peace, and Rev. Dr. David D. Grafton of Lutheran Theological Seminary in Philadelphia.

Ellison, Turkey, and the U.S. Council of Muslim Organizations

The United States Council of Muslim Organizations (USCMO), founded in early 2014, is a political umbrella organization that counts among its core membership many of the top front groups of the Muslim Brotherhood in America. CAIR and its Executive Director, Nihad Awad, play the leading role within the USCMO. In a development that must be monitored with deep concern, the USCMO and the pro-HAMAS regime of Turkish President Recep Tayyip Erdogan are working closely together in the U.S. itself as well as by way of reciprocal visits to both Turkey and the U.S.

Following the formation of the USCMO and shortly after its non-publicized inaugural banquet which was attended by U.S. Congressmen Keith Ellison (Democrat, Minnesota, 5th District) in June 2014, a leadership delegation of U.S. Muslim Brotherhood leaders traveled to Ankara, Turkey, at the invitation of the Turkish government in August 2014. It is notable that this U.S. Congressman is not only working actively with the Muslim Brotherhood, but also is a contributor to programs[152] held by the pro-HAMAS Turkish government-owned Diyanet Center of America in Lanham, Maryland. Even before the official opening of the DCA in April 2016, Ellison was a keynote speaker[153] at a gathering just outside of Washington, D.C. of international Muslim Brotherhood leadership, which included high level party officials from President Recep Tayyip Erdogan's AK Party.

Interesting insight may be gleaned from an excerpt taken from a firsthand account[154] by AKP Member of Parliament Yasin Aktay, who publicly acknowledged the leadership roles of USCMO Secretary General Oussama Jammal and CAIR National Executive Director Nihad Awad, with whom Ellison has a close working relationship. Aktay attended the USCMO's 1st International Conference of Muslim Councils of the West in Washington, DC, from 1-3 February 2016, held at a Crystal City, Virginia, hotel and published online his observations of the event. His details not only confirm the strategic relationship between the USCMO and AKP, but also acknowledge the "connection into an opportunity, a political coalition for Turkey and the Muslim world," as described by Aktay.

This early 2016 gathering, at which Ellison was featured as a keynote speaker, represented an assembly of the international Muslim Brotherhood leadership from over two dozen countries to discuss strategy for addressing challenges in the West and its operational plans for the continuation of Civilization Jihad. Most striking, this event marked a strategic move by Erdoğan to assert his leadership on the international stage and begin providing directives for the work of global Islamic Movement. Here, we see NATO "ally" Turkey spreading its influence and beginning to work with international Muslim Brotherhood leaders on an agenda aligned with the OIC.

Chapter Eight

Straddling the Radical Left and the Islamic Movement

National Muslim Democratic Council

Both the radical left and the American Islamic movements have been increasingly involved in Democratic Party politics in recent years. Straddling both worlds as he does, Keith Ellison is well-placed to broker an alliance between the two anti-American factions.[155]

Muslim Representatives Keith Ellison and Andre Carson, together with Steve Israel, then-chairman of the Democratic Congressional Campaign Committee, sponsored an evening event May 16, 2012 in Washington D.C.

CAIR Executive Director Nihad Awad played a key role in organizing the event.

House Minority Leader Nancy Pelosi headlined the highly confidential gathering.

Present were about 20 members of a Syrian dissident group and 10 officials representing Muslim Brotherhood and Hamas front groups. Council on American-Islamic Relations.

Jamal Barzinji, who died in September 2015, was also in attendance. Barzinji was a founding father of the Muslim Brotherhood in America and co-founder of the Muslim Student Association, an "incubator for Islamic radicalism in North America."

Barzinji was named in a federal affidavit as being closely associated with Palestinian Islamic Jihad and Hamas. His name was found in a global phone book of Muslim Brotherhood members recovered by Italian and Swiss authorities in November 2001 from the home of Al-Taqwa Bank of Lugano founder Youssef Nada, one of the leaders of the international Muslim Brotherhood.

Nancy Pelosi sat at the same table with Awad and Barzinji.

Pelosi told the assembly that the Democratic Party should become the natural home of Muslim-Americans, because Republicans fan the flames of "Islamophobia."

Also speaking were Israel, Ellison, Carson, and Chris Murphy, D-Connecticut—elected to the US Senate later that year. Senator Murphy has well-documented ties to both CAIR and the Communist Party USA.[156] Murphy even employed Communist Party member Max Goldman as a senior Outreach Assistant.[157],[158]

Following the speeches, a prominent attorney, Mazen Asbahi publicly rose to announce the creation of a new organization called the National Muslim Democratic Council (NMDC).

Asbahi had been President Obama's 2008 Muslim outreach director, but was forced to step down when his prior association with a radical Muslim cleric, Jamal Said, became public. Said was named by the Department of Justice as an unindicted co-conspirator in the Holy Land Foundation terrorism financing trial.

The National Muslim Democratic Council seeks to "maximize American Muslim support for Democratic candidates and policies."

A memo detailing the creation and agenda of the National Muslim Democratic Council that is marked "CONFIDENTIAL: NOT FOR PUBLIC DISTRIBUTION" was leaked. In the section marked "2012 election strategy" the group specifically spelled out detailed plans to support the Democrats and target Republicans in "key races where American Muslims can make a difference."[159]

According to the document, these races included:

- Defeating Rep. Allen West, R-Fla., in his race against Patrick Murphy, D-Fla.;
- Supporting former Governor Tim Kaine, D-Virginia., in his race against former Sen. George Allen, in the race for Virginia's vacant Senate seat;
- Supporting Senator Debbie Stabenow, D-Michigan., in her bid for re-election against former House Intelligence Committee Chairman Pete Hoekstra'; and

- Supporting Joyce Beatty, D-Ohio, in her bid to capture the state's 3rd congressional district.

The newly formed Council achieved all its electoral goals.

The confidential NMDC document was signed by several known Islamists such as Jamiah Adams, Jihad Williams, Zeba Iqbal, Assad Akhter, Mazen Asbahi, CAIR's Basim Elkarra; and Linda Sarsour of the Arab American Association of New York.

Linda Sarsour recently joined Democratic Socialists of America.

Linda Sarsour Tweet via Twitter (*Screenshot*)

Gaza, Qatar, and Egypt

Representative Ellison sometimes acted as a sort of unofficial ambassador from the Obama Administration to the Muslim world.

Keith Ellison travelled to Gaza on February 19, 2009 with then-Senator John Kerry (D-Massachusetts), among others. This visit, which did not have the official sanction of the Obama Administration, was the first time anyone from the U.S. government entered Gaza in more than three years.

Andrew Whitley, director of the New York Representative Office of the United Nations Relief and Works Agency (UNRWA), helped organize the visit, where participants were given briefings on "the devastation in Gaza."[160] One of the speakers was Samer Badawi, director of "United Palestinian Appeal, a Palestinian-American charity established in 1978." He claimed that the United States government "questions every act of charity in Palestine, and accuses even UNRWA of aiding and abetting terror." Badawi was quoted as further making the claim that "[E]veryone in Gaza is suspect and presumed guilty until proven innocent."

On January 27, 2010, U.S. Representatives Keith Ellison and ultra-left Washington representative Jim McDermott led 52 other members of Congress in signing a letter addressed to President Barack Obama, calling for him to use diplomatic pressure to resolve the blockade affecting Gaza.[161] The Brotherhood-affiliated Muslim Public Affairs Council (MPAC) praised the effort, using the occasion to promote a "white paper"[162] which concluded that Hamas and Israel were both guilty of "war crimes."

Ellison also flew to Qatar February 2009, to give a speech at Qatar University in the capital city of Doha.[163]

> "Following 9/11, there has been an emergence of Muslim civil rights organizations," Ellison said during the Feb. 15, 2009 address at Qatar University's College of Sharia and Islamic Studies. "The political picture is bright, not perfect, but we are ready to expand the dialogue and work to resolving the

miscomprehensions that exist in our society and between the U.S. and the Islamic world."

"This is the first time a U.S. president has reached out in this way," said Ellison, citing Obama's decision to close Guantanamo Bay, end the war in Iraq and stop using torture. "President Obama's granting his first international interview to Al-Arabiya was a significant move which showed his commitment to his pledge. He was talking straight to Muslims all over the world."

Shortly after the Muslim Brotherhood gained power in Egypt in 2011, Nancy Pelosi led a delegation to Egypt which included Keith Ellison. They met with Field Marshal Hussein Tantawi and other high-ranking Egyptians.[164]

Ellison wrote about the occasion:[165]

While there, we met with members of parliament. Some of my friends from Egypt arranged for me to speak at the Medical Syndicate, a regular town hall forum. I walked into a room of three hundred people...There were many Americans who were happy to see the Egyptian revolution take place...

In addition to Leader Pelosi, other Members of the Congressional delegation were: Congressman George Miller of California, Congressman Ed Markey of Massachusetts, Congressman Nick Rahall of West Virginia, and Congresswoman Carolyn Maloney of New York.

Democratic Platform Drafting Committee

In May 2016, Bernie Sanders supporters Dr. Cornel West and Rep. Keith Ellison (D-Minn.) were among those appointed to the Democratic Party's important Platform Drafting Committee, after the Vermont Senator "won a key concession as he looks to leave his mark on the party's platform".

To heal the very deep divide between Sanders and Clinton supporters, Democratic party officials agreed that Sanders would have five supporters on the committee, compared to six for Hillary Clinton.

Sanders previously had previously attacked DNC Chairwoman Debbie Wasserman Schultz for failing to include enough of his supporters on an initial list. But the latest statement notes that Wasserman Schultz allocated the campaign's seats "proportionally according to the current vote tally."

Dr. Cornel West has been a long-time member of Democratic Socialists of America.[166]

Sanders supporters on the committee included far left environmental leader Bill McKibben, and Arab American Institute head James Zogby, once a senior adviser to Jesse Jackson's Rainbow Coalition.[167]

Clinton loyalists on the committee included former Clinton staffer and current Center for American Progress head Neera Tanden, Socialist International activist and former Obama appointee Carol Browner, far left Illinois Rep. Luis Gutierrez and AFCSME leader. and longtime Democratic Socialists of America member Paul Booth.[168,169]

The socialist fix was in.

In an article titled "Bernie Sanders moved Democrats to the left. The platform is proof" From Vox:[170]

> Hillary Clinton may have won the Democratic Party's presidential nomination, but Bernie Sanders has still left an outsize mark on its future.
>
> Back in July, Sanders won a string of concessions on the Democratic Party platform, pulling the party to the left on the minimum wage, environmental regulation, marijuana legalization, and the war on drugs.
>
> "I think if you read the platform right now, you will understand that the political revolution is alive and kicking," Sanders's policy director, Warren Gunnels, told NBC News at the time, adding that campaign got "at least 80 percent" of what it wanted.

With two far leftists, Keith Ellison and Thom Perez, now leading the Democratic National Committee, there is no reason to believe that the Democratic Party will be heading back to the political center anytime soon, and until Americans demand security clearances from their elected officials, it is likely that subversive elements in high office will continue to wreak havoc with American sovereignty and security.

Chapter Nine

'Enemies foreign and domestic ...'

The United States today faces an intelligence threat that is far more complex than it has ever been historically. The threat is increasingly asymmetrical insofar as it seeks to exploit the areas where there is a perception of weakness within the U.S. national security approach and organizations ...Traditional notions of counterintelligence that focus on hostile foreign INTELLIGENCE *services targeting classified national defense information simply do not reflect the realities of today's complex international structure...While traditional adversaries were limited to centrally controlled national intelligence services,* **today's adversaries include not only these traditional services but also non-traditional and non-state actors who operate from decentralized organizations.**

> —*Kenneth H. Senser, Assistant Director, Security Division, FBI, before the United States Senate, Committee on the Judiciary, Washington, D.C., April 09, 2002*

The U.S. military oath commands all who join to swear to defend the Constitution from "all enemies, foreign and domestic." While the United States has fought, and still is fighting, many costly wars against "foreign enemies," domestic enemies are rarely regarded as a significant national security threat.

Certainly, no-one in the US Congress has been charged with being a domestic threat in recent memory. This may not be because there have been no security risks in Congress, however, but rather because *the FBI has a policy of not investigating serving members of the House of Representatives.*

Shortly after World War II, FBI Director J. Edgar Hoover questioned one of his own officials, D. M. Ladd, why radical New York Congressman Vito Marcantonio's name was not included in the Security Index, a list of Americans to be interned if the Attorney General declared a national emergency.

Ladd replied:

> "...our files fail to disclose any evidence to establish direct proof of Marcantonio's membership in the Communist Party. It has been the practice of the Bureau not to institute security investigations on members of the U.S. Congress. In view of this, Marcantonio has not been considered for inclusion in the Security Index. It should be noted that Marcantonio is running for reelection this November. It is contemplated that should he be defeated; the Bureau would actively investigate him and consider including his name in the Security Index."

In other words, while you're serving, you're safe.

While American government employees can be subject to very rigorous background checks, members of Congress, even those serving on the House Armed Services, Homeland Security and sensitive Intelligence committees are not subject to even the most basic scrutiny.

Is it possible that America's enemies, foreign and domestic, might be aware of this anomaly? Might they even try to exploit these "areas where there is a perception of weakness"?

Former House Intelligence Committee Chairman Pete Hoekstra (Republican Party—Michigan 2) told the author that members of his committee were not subject to background checks at all. Bear in mind that the Intelligence Committee has oversight over the CIA, FBI, NSA, DEA and twelve other intelligence agencies, and additionally has insight into some of America's most valuable secrets, and most carefully guarded strategic plans.

It is difficult to imagine that Representative Keith Ellison would pass any level security clearance investigation. Isn't it fortunate for him that he doesn't have to—perhaps less fortunate for those Americans whom he supposedly represents.

Fighting on new terrain

Representative Keith Ellison is leaving Congress.

On 5 June 2018, Rep. Keith Ellison made a last-minute entry into the Attorney General's race in Minnesota. Ellison announced his candidacy on the final day of filing and one day after the Democratic incumbent, Lori Swanson, announced she would run for governor, thereby opening up the Attorney General's race.

In his public statement, Ellison said he would continue a tradition of fighting for his constituents if elected to the new post.

"Our Pledge of Allegiance promises an America with liberty and justice for all—no exceptions," Ellison said. "But too often, Minnesota's working families and the most vulnerable among us are taken advantage of or are targets of discrimination. I am running to be the People's Lawyer to hold those in power accountable and to protect and defend all Minnesotans."

But on 3 January 2018, Keith Ellison had tweeted a photo of himself holding Mark Bray's book "Antifa: The Anti-Fascist Handbook." He tweeted:

"At @MoonPalaceBooks and I just found the book that strike (sic) fear in the heart of @realDonaldTrump"

Mark Bray explains in his book "Antifa: The Anti-Fascist Handbook" that the "goal" is to completely alienate anyone who voted for President Donald Trump:

"Our goal should be that in twenty years those who voted for Trump are too uncomfortable to share that fact in public. We may not always be able to change someone's beliefs, but we sure as hell can make it politically, socially, economically, and sometimes physically costly to articulate them."

How is this consistent with a pledge to "to protect and defend all Minnesotans"?

Then, in July 2018, Ellison wrote a letter to Amazon CEO Jeff Bezos, demanding Amazon cease selling items that Ellison personally deemed "hateful":

> *"I would like to know whether Amazon is committed to ceasing the sale of all products that promote hateful and racist ideologies," wrote Ellison. "For a company with a policy prohibiting the sale of 'products that promote or glorify hatred, violence, racial, sexual, or religious intolerance or promote organizations with such views,' there appear to be a disturbing number of groups with hateful, racist, and violent agendas making money using Amazon's platform."*[171]

How could an Attorney General Keith Ellison be trusted to "protect and defend" the First Amendment rights of "all Minnesotans" with such a perspective?

Would Attorney General Ellison use his position to advocate for black "reparations," push for tough hate-speech laws, or promote some form of separate Islamic jurisprudence, or even sharia courts in the state?

Judging by the history of his own public statements, the troubling answer to all of these may be "Yes."

Keith Ellison may be leaving Congress, but there is no indication he will be leaving activism.

APPENDIX A

Keith Ellison: Speaking Engagements with Muslim Brotherhood Front Organizations

14 October 2006: Keith Ellison was the keynote speaker at a closed-door meeting of CAIR in Pembroke Pines, Florida.[2]

19 November 2006: Ellison addressed North American Imam Federation conference[3]

"He also addressed the North American Imams Federation (NAIF) at their November 19, 2006 conference in Minneapolis.[4] Many of NAIF's imams, in charge of mosques across the United States, are trained through an institution called the American Open University (AOU), a distance-learning medium for Muslims wishing to train as clergy. The AOU is a radical school that emphasizes the paramount role of Shari'a law in an American context. Its chairman Jaafar Sheikh Idris regards democracy as "the antithesis of Islam," arguing that human beings have no right to make their own laws. "No one," he claims, "can be a Muslim who makes or freely accepts or believes that anyone has the right to make or accept legislation that is contrary to the divine law."[5] He also declared that no Muslim elected to Congress can swear to uphold the U.S. Constitution and remain a Muslim "for in order to pledge loyalty to the constitution, a Muslim would have to abandon part of his belief and embrace the belief of secularism—which is practically another religion."[6] That Keith Ellison supports an institution linked to someone who holds views in such deep conflict with normative American values is deeply troubling."

---

[2] https://www.meforum.org/articles/2010/keith-ellison-s-stealth-jihad#_ftn49
[3] https://www.meforum.org/articles/2010/keith-ellison-s-stealth-jihad
[4] https://www.meforum.org/articles/2010/keith-ellison-s-stealth-jihad#_ftn71
[5] https://www.meforum.org/articles/2010/keith-ellison-s-stealth-jihad#_ftn72
[6] https://www.meforum.org/articles/2010/keith-ellison-s-stealth-jihad#_ftn73

December 2006: Ellison spoke at 6th annual MPAC Convention

December 2006: Ellison spoke at MAS-ICNA Convention in Dearborn, MI

"Ellison, for his part, sounded a defiant note[7] in an address in Dearborn, Michigan. To cries of "Allahu akbar" from a Muslim crowd, he declared: "On January 4, I will go swear an oath to uphold the Constitution of the United States. I'll place my hand on the Quran." Ellison said these words at a convention hosted by the Muslim American Society and the Islamic Circle of North America."[8]

4 January 2007: U.S. representative Keith Ellison placed his hand on an English translation of the Qur'an once owned by Thomas Jefferson, when he was sworn in as the first Muslim member of Congress by Speaker of the House Nancy Pelosi on Capitol Hill, Washington, D.C.

Summer of 2007: Ellison joined CAIR in seeking public support for convicted Palestinian Islamic Jihad (PIJ) supporter Sami Al-Arian saying: "[the Al-Arian family is] working on his case, trying to get some attention from members of Congress, I'm speaking with them and I hope others do as well."[9]

2007: Ellison was guest speaker at ISNA Convention[10]

October 2007: CAIR-Florida's (CAIR-FL) 5th Annual Banquet, held at the Tampa Convention Center, featured a video message in which Ellison offered support for CAIR's mission of engaging the community in conversation about Muslim issues."[11]

17 November 2007: Ellison appeared live and delivered a speech a month later at the CAIR-National 13th Annual Banquet. He specifically thanked CAIR's co-founder and current national Executive Director Nihad Awad, for being present at the local chapter's banquet.[12]

August 2008: Ellison was guest speaker at ISNA's Annual Convention[13] where he discussed effective strategies for the

---

[7] http://www.freep.com/apps/pbcs.dll/article?AID=/20061225/NEWS99/61225002
[8] http://archive.frontpagemag.com/readArticle.aspx?ARTID=867
[9] https://www.investigativeproject.org/791/congress-cozying-up-to-cair
[10] https://www.meforum.org/articles/2010/keith-ellison-s-stealth-jihad
[11] https://www.investigativeproject.org/791/congress-cozying-up-to-cair
[12] https://www.investigativeproject.org/791/congress-cozying-up-to-cair
[13] https://www.meforum.org/articles/2010/keith-ellison-s-stealth-jihad

community-based political advocacy necessary to mobilize the Muslim political machine in the U.S.

24 September of 2008: Ellison was prominent at CAIR-Minnesota's (CAIR-MN) Second Annual Ramadan Dinner.[14]

26 September 2008: Ellison joined CAIR-MI's Dawud Walid in a panel at the Annual Legislative Conference of the Congressional Black Caucus Foundation in Washington D.C.[15]

2008 before Election: Ellison addressed a town hall forum during MPAC's "Activate '08 Election Campaign," at one of the Council's "Rock the Muslim Vote" events[16]

24 November 2008: While attending CAIR-Tampa's sixth annual banquet in 2008, Ellison called on listeners to a local Tampa radio station to support Sami al-Arian. Arian, a former professor at University of South Florida, confessed two years earlier to conspiring to supply goods and services to Palestinian Islamic Jihad, a terrorist organization responsible for numerous suicide attacks on Israel.[17]

December 2008: Ellison took hajj, where MAS-Minnesota paid for him to make a 16-day pilgrimage to Mecca. He was joined on the trip by Asad Zaman, who sits on the board of the Muslim American Society's Minnesota chapter. Zaman has contributed thousands[18] of dollars to Ellison's congressional runs, both before and after the Mecca trip.[19]

2009: Ellison was guest speaker at ISNA Convention[20]

2009: Ellison campaigned for a Libya-born activist Esam Omeish who once called on Palestinians to embrace "the jihad way" in order to get free of Israeli control. Omeish, a former candidate for Virginia state delegate, has also praised one of the founders of Hamas and commended the work of Palestinian suicide bombers. Omeish's

---

[14] https://www.cair.com/cair_mn_second_annual_ramadan_dinner_a_success

[15] https://www.investigativeproject.org/791/congress-cozying-up-to-cair

[16] https://www.meforum.org/articles/2010/keith-ellison-s-stealth-jihad#_ftn70

[17] https://www.meforum.org/articles/2010/keith-ellison-s-stealth-jihad#_ftn50

[18] https://www.opensecrets.org/indivs/search.php?name=zaman%2C+asad&cycle=All&sort=R&state=&zip=&employ=&cand=ellison&submit=Submit

[19] http://www.foxnews.com/politics/2016/11/22/muslim-brotherhood-tied-group-paid-for-keith-ellison-to-visit-mecca-in-2008.html

[20] https://www.meforum.org/articles/2010/keith-ellison-s-stealth-jihad

positions had been publicized when Ellison, the first Muslim ever elected to Congress, headlined the July 2009 fundraiser for Omeish, who served as president from 2004 to 2008 of the Muslim American Society, a Muslim Brotherhood-linked group.[21]

18 September 2009: Ellison spoke to audience of 300 people at CAIR Arizona dinner at the Hilton Phoenix in East Mesa. "I would never associate myself with anyone even soft on terrorism," he said before the speech. "We all want to fight terror. We all want to live in a safe community."[22]

Tuesday, 10 June 2014: Ellison was keynote speaker at United States Council of Muslim Organizations Inaugural Banquet[23]

Monday – Wednesday, 1-3 February 2016: Ellison was keynote speaker during the USCMO 1st International Conference of Muslim Councils of the West[24]

2 March 2016: Ellison addresses audience at Diyanet Center of America[25]

September 2016: Ellison spoke at ISNA convention[26]

7 May 2018: Ellison spoke at Diyanet Center of America[27]

---

[21] http://dailycaller.com/2016/11/21/keith-ellison-headlined-fundraiser-for-muslim-activist-who-called-for-palestinians-to-embrace-the-jihad-way/?utm_campaign=atdailycaller&utm_source=Twitter&utm_medium=Social

[22] http://archive.azcentral.com/arizonarepublic/local/articles/2009/09/19/20090919ellison0919.html#ixzz5HlsVrD24

[23] https://www.centerforsecuritypolicy.org/2014/06/30/u-s-muslim-brotherhood-political-party-convenes-for-inaugural-banquet-in-washington-dc-area/ and http://www.muslimlinkpaper.com/community-news/community-news/3679-new-umbrella-group-holds-inaugural-banquet.html

[24] http://www.muslimlinkpaper.com/community-news/4106-leaders-say-coordinating-council-needed-for-muslims-of-the-western-world

[25] http://www.musiad.us/musiad-usa-met-with-rep-keith-ellison-and-rep-andre-carson/

[26] http://www.isna.net/wp-content/uploads/2016/09/53_convention_program_16_web__1_.pdf

[27] https://www.facebook.com/events/358150908008915/ and http://pgcmcmd.nationbuilder.com/2018_community_discussion

APPENDIX B

Contributions to Rep. Keith Ellison 2006-2017

The following table documents 560 financial contributions made to Rep. Keith Ellison by individuals associated with one or more Muslim Brotherhood (MB) front groups for the period 2006-2017. All donation amounts are reported with a high degree of accuracy except for those marked with an asterisk (*), which denotes a medium level of accuracy. All amounts in US dollars.

Source: Islamist Money in Politics Project (IMIP)

DATE	DONOR	MB GROUP	DONATION
4/24/06	Esam Omeish	CAIR, MAS	500
7/22/06	Samir Abo-Issa	MAS	500
7/22/06	Nihad Awad	CAIR	2000
7/23/06	Corey Saylor	CAIR	1000
7/25/06	Parvez Ahmed	CAIR	250
8/7/06	Parvez Ahmed	CAIR	250
8/11/06	Ghulam Warriach	CAIR	250
8/19/06	Asad Zaman	MAS	1000
8/23/06	Mohamed Ghabour	CAIR	999
8/28/06	James Yee	CAIR	1000
8/29/06	Esam Omeish	CAIR, MAS	500
9/12/06	Hyder Ali	CAIR	1000
9/24/06	Yahya Basha	MPAC	300
10/6/06	Yaqub Mirza	SAAR, SAFA	500
10/16/06	Raza Ali	CAIR	250
10/16/06	Mohamed Ghabour	CAIR	500
10/16/06	Mohamed Ghabour	CAIR	1500
10/16/06	Atif Fareed	CAIR	2100

Date	Donor	MB Group	Donation
10/16/06	Ezzat Zaki	CAIR	1000
10/16/06	Suhail Nanji	CAIR	1000
10/17/06	Parvez Ahmed	CAIR	250
10/19/06	Asad Zaman	MAS	400
10/23/06	Yahya Basha	MPAC	500
10/23/06	Sherif Gindy	CAIR	300
10/23/06	Jukaku Tayeb	CAIR	500
10/25/06	CAIR-CA PAC	CAIR	5000
10/28/06	Rizwan Jaka	CAIR, ISNA	250
10/29/06	Shafath Syed	CAIR	250
10/29/06	Razi Mohiuddin	CAIR	2000
10/29/06	Manzoor Ghori	CAIR, ISNA	500
10/31/06	Muhammad Saleem	CAIR	250*
10/31/06	Muhammad Saleem	CAIR	250*
1/8/07	Muhamad Albadawi	MAS	1000*
1/8/07	Esam Omeish	CAIR, MAS	1000
3/30/07	Yahya Basha	MPAC	500
4/20/07	Zaher Sahloul	CAIR	1000
4/20/07	Mazen Kudaimi	CAIR	1000
5/4/07	Shaukat Gaziani	CAIR	250
5/4/07	Azhar Azeez	CAIR, ISNA, NAIT	500
5/4/07	Ghulam Warriach	CAIR	300
6/30/07	Muzammil Ahmed	CAIR	250
6/30/07	Sherif Gindy	CAIR	250
7/24/07	Razi Mohiuddin	CAIR	2000
7/24/07	Fouad Khatib	CAIR	250
7/24/07	Khaldoon Abugharbieh	CAIR	250
7/25/07	Athar Siddiqee	CAIR	1000
8/27/07	Mohammad Jadid	CAIR	250
8/27/07	Samir Mokaddem	CAIR	300
9/4/07	Muzammil Ahmed	CAIR	400
11/6/07	CAIR-CA PAC	CAIR	5000
11/12/07	Nayyer Ali	MPAC	2300

Date	Donor	MB Group	Donation
11/21/07	Esam Omeish	CAIR, MAS	450
11/30/07	Parvez Ahmed	CAIR	500
12/1/07	Mujeeb Qadri	CAIR	300
12/1/07	Raza Ali	CAIR	250
12/1/07	Mohamed Ghabour	CAIR	2300
12/1/07	Atif Fareed	CAIR	2300
12/2/07	Asad Ba-Yunus	ISNA	250
12/2/07	Syed Ali Rahman	CAIR	300
12/2/07	Suhail Nanji	CAIR	500
12/2/07	Rashid Abbara	CAIR	2000
12/5/07	Tahra Goraya	CAIR	250
12/17/07	Yaqub Mirza	SAAR, SAFA	1000
2/1/08	Magdy Eletreby	MPAC	2300
2/18/08	Hany Elkordy	CAIR	250
2/18/08	Hyder Ali	CAIR	1000
2/18/08	James Yee	CAIR	500
3/1/08	Rizwan Jaka	CAIR, ISNA	500
3/11/08	Aliya Latif	CAIR	400
3/11/08	Dalia Mahmoud	MPAC	500
3/14/08	Zead Ramadan	CAIR	1200
3/15/08	Malik Sarwar	CAIR, MPAC	1000*
4/7/08	Mazen Kudaimi	CAIR	1000
4/7/08	Zaher Sahloul	CAIR	1000
4/14/08	Karen Dabdoub	CAIR	250
5/19/08	Asad Zaman	MAS	300
6/2/08	Yaqub Mirza	SAAR, SAFA	500
6/30/08	Hind Jarrah	CAIR	500
7/11/08	Dalia Mahmoud	MPAC	500
7/28/08	Asad Malik	CAIR	1000
7/28/08	Jukaku Tayeb	CAIR	1000
7/31/08	Haaris Ahmad	CAIR	205
7/31/08	Muzammil Ahmed	CAIR	1000
8/4/08	Haaris Ahmad	CAIR	312

Date	Donor	MB Group	Donation
8/6/08	Muna Jondy	MPAC	2300
8/6/08	Jawad Shah	ISNA, MSA	2300
8/19/08	Suzanne Akhras Sahloul	CAIR	1000
8/19/08	Hesham Hassaballa	CAIR	500
8/20/08	Zaher Sahloul	CAIR	500
9/2/08	Mohammed Alo	CAIR	250*
9/3/08	Osama Idlibi	ISNA, MAS	250
9/8/08	Tarek Hussein	CAIR	500
9/8/08	Tarek Hussein	CAIR	500
9/19/08	Esam Omeish	CAIR, MAS	500
9/26/08	Nasir Mahmood	CAIR	250
9/29/08	Zead Ramadan	CAIR	1000
10/17/08	Yaqub Mirza	SAAR, SAFA	1000
10/20/08	Safaa Ibrahim	CAIR	300
10/20/08	Fouad Khatib	CAIR	200
10/20/08	Shafath Syed	CAIR	500
10/20/08	Athar Siddiqee	CAIR	250
10/20/08	Razi Mohiuddin	CAIR	1000
10/27/08	Jamal Barzinji	IIIT, ISNA, MSA, NAIT, SAAR, SAFA	500
10/31/08	Yahya Basha	MPAC	300
11/17/08	Mohamed Ghabour	CAIR	500
11/17/08	Atif Fareed	CAIR	500
11/25/08	Nazir Hamoui	CAIR	1000
2/28/09	Ahsan Ahmed	CAIR	500
2/28/09	Omar Hassaine	CAIR	500
2/28/09	Owais Siddiqui	CAIR	500
3/16/09	Yahya Basha	MPAC	500
3/16/09	Muzammil Ahmed	CAIR	500
6/1/09	Usama Gabr	CAIR	250*
6/13/09	Rizwan Jaka	CAIR, ISNA	250
6/15/09	Magdy Eletreby	MPAC	500
6/17/09	Esam Omeish	CAIR, MAS	500

Date	Donor	MB Group	Donation
7/3/09	Kenan Basha	ISNA, MSA	250
7/9/09	Asad Malik	CAIR	250
7/21/09	Elijah Muhammad	CAIR	250
7/21/09	Zead Ramadan	CAIR	1000
7/21/09	Maher El Jamal	MAS	300
7/21/09	Wael Hamza	MAS	250
7/21/09	Dalia Mahmoud	MPAC	700
8/20/09	Suhail Nanji	CAIR	25
9/14/09	Suhail Nanji	CAIR	1000
9/21/09	Mannan Mohammed	CAIR	500
9/21/09	Mohamed El-Sharkawy	CAIR	500
9/28/09	Zead Ramadan	CAIR	250
12/1/09	Hind Jarrah	CAIR	500
12/7/09	Jamal Barzinji	IIIT, ISNA, MSA, NAIT, SAAR, SAFA	250
12/14/09	Safaa Zarzour	CAIR, ISNA	250
1/26/10	Asad Zaman	MAS	250
2/8/10	Jamal Barzinji	IIIT, ISNA, MSA, NAIT, SAAR, SAFA	500
3/24/10	Zead Ramadan	CAIR	250
3/24/10	Zead Ramadan	CAIR	500
3/26/10	Aly Abuzaakouk	AMC, IIIT, UASR	250
3/26/10	Hisham Altalib	IIIT, SAAR, SAFA	1000
3/26/10	Esam Omeish	CAIR, MAS	500
4/13/10	Emad Hamwi	CAIR	300
4/21/10	Dalia Mahmoud	MPAC	1000
5/12/10	Dalia Mahmoud	MPAC	500
5/18/10	Zaid Abdur-Rahman	CAIR	300
5/24/10	Safaa Zarzour	CAIR, ISNA	500
5/24/10	Ahmed Rehab	CAIR	250
5/24/10	Mazen Kudaimi	CAIR	2000
5/24/10	Emad Hamwi	CAIR	200
6/10/10	Asad Zaman	MAS	500

Date	Donor	MB Group	Donation
6/11/10	Rashid Abbara	CAIR	1000
6/29/10	Zead Ramadan	CAIR	400
6/29/10	Zead Ramadan	CAIR	600
6/29/10	Suzanne Akhras Sahloul	CAIR	500
6/30/10	Azeez Farooki	MPAC	500
6/30/10	Dalia Mahmoud	MPAC	200
6/30/10	Dalia Mahmoud	MPAC	1300
6/30/10	Safaa Zarzour	CAIR, ISNA	500
8/30/10	Mohamed El-Sharkawy	CAIR	100
9/27/10	Nayyer Ali	MPAC	2400
10/11/10	Esam Omeish	CAIR, MAS	250
10/15/10	Yaqub Mirza	SAAR, SAFA	500
10/19/10	Rizwan Jaka	CAIR, ISNA	300
11/1/10	Dalia Mahmoud	MPAC	1100
1/26/11	Naveen Bhora	MPAC	500
1/26/11	Athar Siddiqee	CAIR	250
1/26/11	Shafath Syed	CAIR	250
2/15/11	Dalia Mahmoud	MPAC	1000
3/16/11	Haaris Ahmad	CAIR	2400
3/16/11	Asad Malik	CAIR	500
3/17/11	Yahya Basha	MPAC	500
3/21/11	Jawad Shah	ISNA, MSA	2000
3/21/11	Mohammed Saleem	CAIR	500
3/31/11	Ashraf Sufi	ISNA	500
5/7/11	Asad Zaman	MAS	200
5/31/11	Zaher Sahloul	CAIR	500
5/31/11	Yaser Tabbara	CAIR	500
6/1/11	Shamel Abd-Allah	CAIR	500
6/21/11	Omar Hassaine	CAIR	250*
9/7/11	Nazir Hamoui	CAIR	1250
10/27/11	Zead Ramadan	CAIR	300
11/7/11	Kenneth Gamble	MANA	1000
11/7/11	Iftekhar Hussain	CAIR	375

Date	Donor	MB Group	Donation
11/30/11	Athar Siddiqee	CAIR	100
11/30/11	Muzammil Ahmed	CAIR	1000
12/5/11	Ahmed Al Shehab	CAIR	300
12/5/11	Samih Abbassi	CAIR	500
12/5/11	Elijah Muhammad	CAIR	250
12/19/11	Suhail Nanji	CAIR	1000
12/19/11	Rashid Abbara	CAIR	500
12/20/11	Khurrum Wahid	CAIR	300
1/28/12	Ahmed Younis	MPAC	250*
3/7/12	Dalia Mahmoud	MPAC	1000
3/12/12	Azeez Farooki	MPAC	500
3/28/12	Zead Ramadan	CAIR	1000
3/30/12	Nasir Mahmood	CAIR	250
4/14/12	Khurrum Wahid	CAIR	500
5/15/12	Mohammed Saleem	CAIR	200
5/15/12	Thasin Sardar	CAIR	250
5/15/12	Muna Jondy	MPAC	1000
6/1/12	Hashem Mubarak	CAIR	250
6/10/12	Jawad Shah	ISNA, MSA	1000
6/12/12	Mohammed Saleem	CAIR	400
6/21/12	Jamal Barzinji	IIIT, ISNA, MSA, NAIT, SAAR, AFA	500
6/24/12	Atif Fareed	CAIR	250
7/9/12	Khalid Siddiq	CAIR	250
7/16/12	Yahya Basha	MPAC	400
7/23/12	Aamna Anwer	MSA	20*
7/25/12	Mudusar Raza	CAIR	200
7/26/12	Zead Ramadan	CAIR	25
8/8/12	Asad Zaman	MAS	250
8/10/12	Azeez Farooki	MPAC	25
8/10/12	Khurrum Wahid	CAIR	250
8/13/12	Rizwan Jaka	CAIR, ISNA	250
8/14/12	Naveen Bhora	MPAC	500
8/18/12	Kenan Basha	ISNA, MSA	250

Date	Donor	MB Group	Donation
8/31/12	Zaher Sahloul	CAIR	500
9/1/12	Hashem Mubarak	CAIR	250
9/4/12	Omar Hassaine	CAIR	100*
9/4/12	Muhammad Saleem	CAIR	100
9/13/12	Nayyer Ali	MPAC	1000
9/17/12	Hashem Mubarak	CAIR	250
9/21/12	Ashraf Sufi	ISNA	1000
9/27/12	Khalique Zahir	ISNA	500
9/30/12	Azeez Farooki	MPAC	25
9/30/12	Azeez Farooki	MPAC	1000
9/30/12	Shafath Syed	CAIR	500
9/30/12	Athar Siddiqee	CAIR	250
10/17/12	Naveen Bhora	MPAC	50
11/2/12	Yaser Tabbara	CAIR	100
11/4/12	Hashem Mubarak	CAIR	250
11/20/12	Naveen Bhora	MPAC	500
12/11/12	Dalia Mahmoud	MPAC	1000
1/17/13	James (Khalil) Meek	CAIR	1000
2/12/13	Arsalan Iftikhar	CAIR	5
3/12/13	Fawzia Keval	CAIR	250
3/12/13	Jeffrey Saladin	CAIR	250
3/15/13	Rashid Ahmad	CAIR	250
3/18/13	Basim Elkarra	CAIR	251
3/18/13	T. Sami Siddiqui	CAIR	250
3/21/13	CAIR-CA PAC	CAIR	500
5/13/13	Asad Zaman	MAS	250
6/24/13	Suhail Nanji	CAIR	500
7/19/13	Akram Elzend	MAS	500
8/5/13	Zead Ramadan	CAIR	500
8/5/13	Maher El Jamal	MAS	400
9/11/13	Akram Elzend	MAS	1000
9/11/13	Hadia Mubarak	CAIR, ISNA, MSA	250
9/13/13	Mazen Kudaimi	CAIR	1000

Date	Donor	MB Group	Donation
9/17/13	Nayyer Ali	MPAC	2500
9/20/13	Hisham Altalib	IIIT, SAAR, SAFA	1000
9/20/13	M. Omar Ashraf	SAFA	1000
9/23/13	Noor Zubeida Khan	MPAC	300
9/26/13	Hashem Mubarak	CAIR	250
9/30/13	Junaid Malik	CAIR	250
9/30/13	Jamal Barzinji	IIIT, ISNA, MSA, NAIT, SAAR, SAFA	1000
10/1/13	Hashem Mubarak	CAIR	100
10/10/13	Esam Omeish	CAIR, MAS	500
10/21/13	Yahya Basha	MPAC	500
10/21/13	Kenan Basha	ISNA, MSA	500
10/24/13	Muzammil Ahmed	CAIR	1000
11/17/13	Ahmed Bedier	CAIR	1000
11/21/13	Amir Khaliq	CAIR	750
11/25/13	Nazir Hamoui	CAIR	250
12/27/13	Hashem Mubarak	CAIR	250
12/31/13	Tarek Hussein	CAIR	1000
12/31/13	Junaid Malik	CAIR	250
1/27/14	Hassan Ahmad	CAIR	400
2/1/14	Hadia Mubarak	CAIR, ISNA, MSA	30
2/1/14	Hadia Mubarak	CAIR, ISNA, MSA	30
2/6/14	Hassan Ahmad	CAIR	500
2/7/14	Ayman Hammous	MAS	250
3/14/14	Hashem Mubarak	CAIR	250
6/8/14	Dalia Mahmoud	MPAC	400
6/8/14	Dalia Mahmoud	MPAC	1600
6/12/14	Muzammil Ahmed	CAIR	500
6/16/14	M. Affan Badar	ISNA	50
6/26/14	Hisham Abdallah	MAS	50
7/22/14	Erfan Obeid	CAIR	250
7/23/14	Asad Zaman	MAS	100
8/1/14	Hadia Mubarak	CAIR, ISNA, MSA	30
8/1/14	Hadia Mubarak	CAIR, ISNA, MSA	30

Date	Donor	MB Group	Donation
8/4/14	Chaudhry Sadiq	CAIR	51
8/12/14	Hassan Ahmad	CAIR	500
8/29/14	Malik Sarwar	CAIR, MPAC	500*
9/8/14	Hussam Ayloush	CAIR	200
9/14/14	Nayyer Ali	MPAC	1000
10/1/14	Shahrukh Jovindah	CAIR	100
10/10/14	M. Affan Badar	ISNA	50
10/20/14	Osama Idlibi	ISNA, MAS	1000
10/23/14	Athar Siddiqee	CAIR	100
10/29/14	Hisham Abdallah	MAS	100
11/2/14	Rizwan Jaka	CAIR, ISNA	100
11/3/14	Kashif Saroya	CAIR	1000
12/18/14	Mohamad Chehade	ISNA	25
1/27/15	Jawad Shah	ISNA, MSA	500
2/2/15	Jawad Shah	ISNA, MSA	500
2/2/15	Mohammed Saleem	CAIR	500
2/23/15	Esam Omeish	CAIR, MAS	250
3/13/15	Hisham Abdallah	MAS	100
3/31/15	Aly Abuzaakouk	AMC, IIIT, UASR	25
3/31/15	Ahlam Jbara	CAIR	50
4/16/15	Junaid Malik	CAIR	250
4/20/15	Osama Al-Qasem	CAIR	100
4/24/15	Iftekhar Hussain	CAIR	500
4/29/15	Hisham Abdallah	MAS	100
4/29/15	Hisham Abdallah	MAS	100
5/1/15	Hashem Mubarak	CAIR	150
5/27/15	Fatima Antar	CAIR	500
8/1/15	Hashem Mubarak	CAIR	150
8/24/15	Mohamad Chehade	ISNA	25
9/12/15	Nayyer Ali	MPAC	2700
9/17/15	Muzammil Ahmed	CAIR	1000
9/27/15	Aly Abuzaakouk	AMC, IIIT, UASR	25
9/30/15	Athar Siddiqee	CAIR	100

Date	Donor	MB Group	Donation
10/26/15	Amina Rab	CAIR	100
11/1/15	Hashem Mubarak	CAIR	150
11/3/15	Ghulam Warriach	CAIR	500
11/18/15	Ahlam Jbara	CAIR	25
11/30/15	Athar Siddiqee	CAIR	100
12/9/15	Valerie Shirley	CAIR	5
12/15/15	Ramzi Mohammad	CAIR	25
1/7/16	Amin Ezzeddine	CAIR, MAS	50
1/10/16	Mohammad Auwal	CAIR	10
1/12/16	Ramzi Mohammad	CAIR	25
1/14/16	Kashif Abdul-Karim	CAIR	10
1/16/16	Mohammad Auwal	CAIR	10
1/25/16	Muhammad Saleem	CAIR	250
1/28/16	Sameena Usman	CAIR	50
1/31/16	Shakeela Hassan	CAIR	100
2/1/16	Owais Siddiqui	CAIR	10
2/7/16	Amin Ezzeddine	CAIR, MAS	50
2/9/16	Shafath Syed	CAIR	500
2/9/16	Shafath Syed	CAIR	1000
2/10/16	Mohammad Auwal	CAIR	10
2/12/16	Ramzi Mohammad	CAIR	25
2/21/16	Iyad Hindi	MAS	25
2/25/16	Tahirah Amatul-Wadud	CAIR	25
3/3/16	Ahmed Azam	MAS	100*
3/7/16	Amin Ezzeddine	CAIR, MAS	50
3/10/16	Mohammad Auwal	CAIR	10
3/12/16	Ramzi Mohammad	CAIR	25
3/13/16	Shakeela Hassan	CAIR	10
3/20/16	Iyad Hindi	MAS	10
3/23/16	Amir Khaliq	CAIR	1000
3/29/16	Ahlam Jbara	CAIR	25
4/10/16	Mohammad Auwal	CAIR	10

Date	Donor	MB Group	Donation
4/13/16	Shakeela Hassan	CAIR	10
4/15/16	Iyad Hindi	MAS	25
4/15/16	Tahirah Amatul-Wadud	CAIR	5
4/26/16	Faroque Khan	ISNA	50
5/2/16	Muzammil Ahmed	CAIR	1000
5/6/16	Hisham Abdallah	MAS	50
5/10/16	Mohammad Auwal	CAIR	10
5/13/16	Shakeela Hassan	CAIR	10
5/16/16	Samir Abo-Issa	MAS	250
5/24/16	Akram Elzend	MAS	1500
5/25/16	Faroque Khan	ISNA	25
5/26/16	Yaqub Mirza	SAAR, SAFA	1000
5/26/16	Esam Omeish	CAIR, MAS	1000
5/28/16	Faroque Khan	ISNA	10
6/6/16	Hisham Abdallah	MAS	50
6/8/16	Faroque Khan	ISNA	50
6/10/16	Mohammad Auwal	CAIR	10
6/15/16	Azeez Farooki	MPAC	1000
6/17/16	M. Affan Badar	ISNA	50
6/25/16	Faroque Khan	ISNA	25
6/30/16	Mohammad Yunus	ICNA	500
7/6/16	Hisham Abdallah	MAS	50
7/10/16	Mohammad Auwal	CAIR	10
7/17/16	Mohammad Assar	CAIR	35
7/25/16	Faroque Khan	ISNA	25
7/30/16	Kashif Abdul-Karim	CAIR	25
8/3/16	Hadi Hassan	CAIR	250
8/6/16	Hisham Abdallah	MAS	50
8/10/16	Mohammad Auwal	CAIR	10
8/25/16	Faroque Khan	ISNA	25
9/6/16	Hisham Abdallah	MAS	50
9/19/16	Nayyer Ali	MPAC	2700
9/25/16	Faroque Khan	ISNA	25

Date	Donor	MB Group	Donation
10/6/16	Hisham Abdallah	MAS	50
10/25/16	Faroque Khan	ISNA	25
10/26/16	Faroque Khan	ISNA	500
11/6/16	Hisham Abdallah	MAS	50
11/15/16	Neekta Hamidi	CAIR	25*
11/20/16	Monem Salam	CAIR, ISNA	500
11/20/16	M. Affan Badar	ISNA	10
11/21/16	Azeez Farooki	MPAC	50
11/21/16	Fawad Shaiq	CAIR	10*
11/22/16	Mujeeb Cheema	CAIR, ISNA, NAIT	25
12/6/16	Hisham Abdallah	MAS	50
12/9/16	Hashem Mubarak	CAIR	50
12/9/16	Valerie Shirley	CAIR	5
12/14/16	Kamal Yassin	CAIR	1000
12/15/16	Kamal Yassin	CAIR	10
12/19/16	Ramzi Mohammad	CAIR	50
12/20/16	Amina Rab	CAIR	5
12/28/16	Hashem Mubarak	CAIR	1000
12/29/16	Ramzi Mohammad	CAIR	100
12/29/16	Kamal Yassin	CAIR	50
1/3/17	Hashem Mubarak	CAIR	50
1/4/17	Ehab Shehata	CAIR	175
1/6/17	Hisham Abdallah	MAS	50
1/7/17	Maaria Mozaffar	CAIR	2700
1/7/17	Bassam Osman	ISNA, NAIT	1000
1/9/17	Valerie Shirley	CAIR	5
1/16/17	Athar Siddiqee	CAIR	500
1/16/17	Athar Siddiqee	CAIR	500
1/19/17	Kashif Abdul-Karim	CAIR	10
1/19/17	Faroque Khan	ISNA	25
1/20/17	Kashif Abdul-Karim	CAIR	10
1/22/17	Muna Jondy	MPAC	1000

Date	Donor	MB Group	Donation
1/31/17	Kamal Yassin	CAIR	1000
2/1/17	Ahmad Al-Akhras	CAIR	250
2/1/17	Ramzi Mohammad	CAIR	50
2/2/17	Dalia Mahmoud	MPAC	1000
2/5/17	Hashem Mubarak	CAIR	1500
2/6/17	Hisham Abdallah	MAS	50
2/9/17	Valerie Shirley	CAIR	5
2/10/17	Hashem Mubarak	CAIR	50
2/12/17	Kenan Basha	ISNA, MSA	1000
2/15/17	Muzammil Ahmed	CAIR	1000
2/17/17	Yasir Mahar	CAIR	25
2/22/17	Mohammad Yunus	ICNA	25
2/22/17	Shahed Amanullah	MPAC	25
2/22/17	Yaqub Mirza	SAAR, SAFA	100
2/23/17	Patricio Pace	CAIR	25
2/24/17	Rashid Ahmad	CAIR	25
2/24/17	Rashid Ahmad	CAIR	25
3/1/17	Ahmad Al-Akhras	CAIR	250
3/3/17	Khalid Abdul-Fatah Griggs	ICNA, MANA	25
3/6/17	Ibrahim Moiz	CAIR	500
3/6/17	Hisham Abdallah	MAS	50
3/6/17	Taher Herzallah	AMP	2500
3/9/17	Valerie Shirley	CAIR	5
3/10/17	Hashem Mubarak	CAIR	50
3/30/17	Aly Abuzaakouk	AMC, IIIT, UASR	25
4/6/17	Hisham Abdallah	MAS	50
4/7/17	Hashem Mubarak	CAIR	50
4/9/17	Valerie Shirley	CAIR	5
4/30/17	Khalid Abdul-Fatah Griggs	ICNA, MANA	25
5/5/17	Hashem Mubarak	CAIR	50
5/6/17	Hisham Abdallah	MAS	50
5/9/17	Valerie Shirley	CAIR	5

Date	Donor	MB Group	Donation
5/15/17	Suzanne Akhras Sahloul	CAIR	1000
6/6/17	Hisham Abdallah	MAS	50
6/9/17	Hashem Mubarak	CAIR	50
6/9/17	Valerie Shirley	CAIR	5
6/30/17	Erfan Obeid	CAIR	250
7/6/17	Hisham Abdallah	MAS	50
7/7/17	Hashem Mubarak	CAIR	50
7/9/17	Valerie Shirley	CAIR	5
7/10/17	Hadi Hassan	CAIR	500
7/27/17	Ramzi Mohammad	CAIR	25
7/31/17	Ahmad Al-Akhras	CAIR	50
8/6/17	Hisham Abdallah	MAS	50
8/9/17	Valerie Shirley	CAIR	5
8/11/17	Hashem Mubarak	CAIR	50
8/27/17	Ramzi Mohammad	CAIR	25
9/8/17	Hashem Mubarak	CAIR	50
9/27/17	Ramzi Mohammad	CAIR	25
10/27/17	Ramzi Mohammad	CAIR	25
11/27/17	Ramzi Mohammad	CAIR	25
		Total	220,493

REFERENCES

[1] Jefferson, Thomas. From Thomas Jefferson to Edward Carrington, 27 May 1788 LINK: https://founders.archives.gov/documents/Jefferson/01-13-02-0120

[2] Ellison, Keith. "My Country, 'Tis of Thee: My Faith, My Family, Our Future," Page 23. Simon and Schuster, Oct 21, 2014

[3] Murphy, Tim. "Keith Ellison Is Everything Republicans Thought Obama Was. Maybe He's Just What Democrats Need," Mother Jones, March/April 2017 Issue LINK: https://www.motherjones.com/politics/2017/02/keith-ellison-democratic-national-committee-chair/

[4] Kaplan, Samuel and Sylvia. "Keith Ellison is the leader the DNC needs," The Hill, December 2016 LINK: http://thehill.com/blogs/pundits-blog/national-party-news/309322-keith-ellison-is-the-leader-the-dnc-needs

[5] Sturdevant, Lori. "How to get out the vote? (Keith Ellison demonstrates.) Star Tribune, Nov 26, 2014 LINK: http://www.startribune.com/how-to-get-out-the-vote-keith-ellison-demonstrates/284044361/

[6] Murphy, Tim. "Keith Ellison Is Everything Republicans Thought Obama Was. Maybe He's Just What Democrats Need," Mother Jones, March/April 2017 Issue LINK: https://www.motherjones.com/politics/2017/02/keith-ellison-democratic-national-committee-chair

[7] Ellison, Keith. "My Country, 'Tis of Thee: My Faith, My Family, Our Future," Page 77-78. Simon and Schuster, Oct 21, 2014

[8] Farrell, John A. "Clarence Darrow: Dragonslayer," History Net, October 29, 2017. LINK: http://www.historynet.com/clarence-darrow-dragonslayer.htm

[9] Stout, David. "William Kunstler, 76, Dies; Lawyer for Social Outcasts," New York Times, August 1995 LINK: https://www.nytimes.com/1995/09/05/obituaries/william-kunstler-76-dies-lawyer-for-social-outcasts.html

[10] Loudon, Trevor, Keywiki Profile George Crockett, Jr. LINK: http://www.keywiki.org/George_Crockett,_Jr.

[11] Loudon, Trevor, Keywiki Profile John Conyers, Jr. LINK: http://www.keywiki.org/John_Conyers,_Jr.

[12] Ellison, Keith. "My Country, 'Tis of Thee: My Faith, My Family, Our Future," Page 77-78. Simon and Schuster, Oct 21, 2014

[13] Garsd, Jasmine. "Rep. André Carson To Become First Muslim On House Committee On Intelligence," NPR (All Things Considered), January 13, 2015. LINK: https://www.npr.org/sections/thetwo-way/2015/01/13/376998473/congressman-andr-carson-to-become-first-muslim-on-house-committee-on-intelligenc

[14] This Far by Faith, "Warith Deen Mohammed," PBS.org. LINK: http://www.pbs.org/thisfarbyfaith/people/warith_deen_mohammed.html

[15] Johnson, Dirk. "Farrakhan Ends Longtime Rivalry with Orthodox Muslims," New York Times, February 28 2000. LINK: https://www.nytimes.com/2000/02/28/us/farrakhan-ends-longtime-rivalry-with-orthodox-muslims.html

[16] Martin, Douglas. "W. Deen Mohammed, 74, Top U.S. Imam, Dies," New York Times, Sept 9 2008. LINK: https://www.nytimes.com/2008/09/10/us/10mohammed.html

[17] Retrieved from WayBack Machine: Warith Deen Muhammad, adapted from entry submitted to Encyclopedia of American Religion and Politics, 2002. (archived) Link: https://web.archive.org/web/20030130081552/http://home.att.net/~spmckee/people_muhammadwd.html

[18] Ellison, Keith. "My Country, 'Tis of Thee: My Faith, My Family, Our Future," Page 88. Simon and Schuster, Oct 21, 2014

[19] Ellison, Keith. "My Country, 'Tis of Thee: My Faith, My Family, Our Future," Page 110. Simon and Schuster, Oct 21, 2014

[20] Ellison, Keith. "My Country, 'Tis of Thee: My Faith, My Family, Our Future," Page 91. Simon and Schuster, Oct 21, 2014

[21] Kessler, Glenn "DNC vice chair Keith Ellison and Louis Farrakhan: 'No relationship'?" Washington Post, March 9, 2018 LINK: https://www.washingtonpost.com/news/fact-checker/wp/2018/03/09/dnc-vice-chair-keith-ellison-and-louis-farrakhan-no-relationship/?utm_term=.bee24108b2a6

[22] Greenfield, Daniel. "KEITH ELLISON'S "PANTS ON FIRE" LIE ABOUT HIS NATION OF ISLAM TIES" FrontPageMag March 18, 2018 LINK: https://www.frontpagemag.com/point/269636/keith-ellisons-pants-fire-lie-about-his-nation-daniel-greenfield

[23] Scheck, Tom. "Keith Ellison dogged by his past. Minnesota Public Radio News June 30, 2006. LINK: https://www.mprnews.org/story/2006/06/22/ellisonprofile

[24] The Final call: "A dialogue with Iran's new president" BY FINALCALL.COM NEWS, OCT 2, 2013. LINK: http://www.finalcall.com/artman/publish/National_News_2/article_100830.shtml

[25] Associated Press, "Perpich asked to intervene in police dispute." St. Cloud Times, St. Cloud, Minnesota. March 24, 1989, Link: https://www.newspapers.com/image/225772059/

[26] Calendar. "Stop Police Brutality from Miami to Minneapolis," The Militant. March 10, 1989. LINK: http://www.themilitant.com/1989/5308/MIL5308.pdf

[27] Star Tribune, 11 Dec 1988, Sun, Page 37

[28] Ellison, Keith. "My Country, 'Tis of Thee: My Faith, My Family, Our Future," Page 125. Simon and Schuster, Oct 21, 2014

[29] "Battling the Rise in Police Brutality." Forward Motion, June 1989 LINK: https://assets.documentcloud.org/documents/3444091/EllisonForwardMotion.pdf

[30] McCartan, Greg. "Support the socialist alternative in 1992!" The Militant, April 10, 1992 LINK: http://www.themilitant.com/1992/5614/MIL5614.pdf

[31] Mgeni, Yusef and August Nimtz. "GRENADA: BLACK REVOLUTION IN THE CARIBBEAN," The Militant, Feb. 20, 1988 LINK: http://www.themilitant.com/1988/5208/MIL5208.pdf

[32] Mgeni, Yusef and August Nimtz. "Malcolm X: the Struggle for Freedom," The Militant, Sept. 21, 1980 LINK: http://www.themilitant.com/1980/4434/MIL4434.pdf

[33] Mgeni, Yusef and August Nimtz, et al. "STOP THE RACIST ATTACKS! RACISM IN AMERICA & MINNESOTA. MULTIPLE MURDERS IN BUFFALO & ATLANTA," The Militant, November 9, 1980 LINK: http://www.themilitant.com/1988/5208/MIL5208.pdf

[34] Mgeni, Yusef and August Nimtz. "STRUGGLE FOR BLACK RIGHTS IN 1981" The Militant, January 18, 1981 LINK: http://www.themilitant.com/1981/4501/MIL4501.pdf

[35] Loudon, Trevor, Keywiki Profile Keith Ellison. LINK: https://keywiki.org/Keith_Ellison

[36] President Bill Clinton's White House Website (archived) "One America: Promising Practices The President's Initiative on Race" LINK: https://clintonwhitehouse3.archives.gov/Initiatives/OneAmerica/Practices/pp_19980804.3503.html

[37] Callaghan, Peter. "A lot of people believe the Twin Cities needs more affordable housing; a lot fewer agree on where to build it," Minnesota Post, November 5, 2015 LINK: https://www.minnpost.com/politics-policy/2015/11/lot-people-believe-twin-cities-needs-more-affordable-housing-lot-fewer-agree

[38] Ellison, Keith. "My Country, 'Tis of Thee: My Faith, My Family, Our Future," Page 99. Simon and Schuster, Oct 21, 2014

39 Postel, Danny. "Solidarity is not a Crime: Statement from the Minnesota Committee in Solidarity with the People of Syria (Minnesota CISPOS)" PulseMedia.org. January 29, 2015. LINK: https://pulsemedia.org/2015/01/29/solidarity-is-not-a-crime-statement-from-the-minnesota-committee-in-solidarity-with-the-people-of-syria-minnesota-cispos/

40 FightBack! News "U.S. progressives meet with Iranian President Mahmoud Ahmadinejad" September 23, 2010. LINK: http://www.fightbacknews.org/2010/9/23/us-progressives-meet-iranian-president-mahmoud-ahmadinejad,

41 Snyders, Matt. "Protest News Anti-War Protesters Gather at State Capitol" CityPages blogs Jul. 9, 2008

[42] Abbas, Roxanne. Minnesota Peace Project, WAMM Newsletter, March 2009.

[43] Report on Congressional Delegation from the Committee to Stop FBI Repression, U.S. Peace Council website, posted Nov. 20, 2010 LINK: http://uspeacecouncil.org/?p=334

[44] The LAWG Cuba Team: Mavis, Emily and Karina "Update on Cuba Travel: We Gathered 59 Signatures" Latin America Working Group, May 03, 2013 LINK: http://www.lawg.org/action-center/78-end-the-embargo-on-cuba/1194-update-on-cuba-travel-we-gathered-59-signatures

[45] Lucom, Wilson C. "Communists in the Democratic Party," Concerned Voters, Inc. 1990 LINK: https://smile.amazon.com/Communists-Democratic-Party-Concerned-

Voters/dp/0962742708/ref=smi_www_rco2_go_smi_g1405964225?_encoding=UTF8&%2AVersion%2A=1&%2Aentries%2A=0&ie=UTF8

[46] Krohnke, Duane W., Minneapolis' Westminster Presbyterian Church's Connections with Cuba, dwkcommentaries. January 13, 2015. LINK: https://dwkcommentaries.com/2015/01/13/minneapolis-westminster-presbyterian-churchs-connections-with-cuba/

[47] Nimtz, August H. "A black socialist in Trump Country,"Star Tribune. July 29, 2016. LINK: http://www.startribune.com/a-black-socialist-in-trump-country/388716201/

[48] Johnson, Scott. "Keith Ellison: Democrat, Nation of Islam follower, Media asks no questions, as usual. With politicians like this, who needs enemies?" Activist Midwest newsletter Aug 28, 2011. LINK: http://actmidwestnews.blogspot.co.nz/2012/01/keith-ellison-democrat-nation-of-islam.html

[49] "Stokely Carmichael" biography, Freedom Riders, American Experience website (PBS). LINK: http://www.pbs.org/wgbh/americanexperience/features/meet-players-freedom-riders/

[50] Kaufman, Michael T. "Stokely Carmichael, Rights Leader Who Coined 'Black Power,' Dies at 57" New York Times, November 16, 1998. LINK: https://www.nytimes.com/1998/11/16/us/stokely-carmichael-rights-leader-who-coined-black-power-dies-at-57.html

[51] Alcindor, Yamiche. "John Conyers to Leave Congress Amid Harassment Claims," New York Times, Dec 5 2017 LINK: https://www.nytimes.com/2017/12/05/us/politics/john-conyers-election.html

[52] Gannon, Francis X. Biographical Dictionary of the Left, Vol. I, page 292, 293, published 1969.

[53] Mosedale, Mike. "Bury My Heart" City Pages News Feb 16, 2000 (archived) LINK: https://web.archive.org/web/20140812214844/http:/www.citypages.com/2000-02-16/news/bury-my-heart/full/

[54] Police Officers Federation of Minneapolis; "MINNEOPOLIS OFFICERS KILLED IN THE LINE OF DUTY," (archived) LINK: https://web.archive.org/web/20070506185807/http://www.mpdfederation.com/jerome-haaf.asp

[55] Court of Appeals, STATE of Minnesota, Respondent, v. Samuel Kenneth WILLIS, Appellant. State v. Willis, February 19, 1985 LINK: https://law.justia.com/cases/minnesota/court-of-appeals/1985/no-0.html

[56] Worthington, Rogers. "In Shadow Of Trial, Faith In Gang Leader Lies Shattered," Chicago Tribune, February 21, 1995. LINK: http://articles.chicagotribune.com/1995-02-21/news/9502220001_1_gang-gambling-dispute-drug-charges

[57] McKinney, MJM. "Officer Jerry Haaf, killed 20 years ago today," Star Tribune, Sept 26, 2012. LINK: http://www.startribune.com/officer-jerry-haaf-killed-20-years-ago-today/171225471/

[58] Supreme Court of Minnesota; STATE of Minnesota, Respondent, v. A.C. FORD, Jr., Appellant. September 1, 1995 LINK: https://law.justia.com/cases/minnesota/supreme-court/1995/c5-93-1872-2.html

[59] Supreme Court of Minnesota, STATE of Minnesota, Respondent, v. Larry Jerome FLOURNOY, Appellant. August 4, 1995 LINK: https://law.justia.com/cases/minnesota/supreme-court/1995/c0-94-316-2.html

[60] Johnson, Scott. "Who is Keith Ellison?" Powerline Blog, June 16, 2006 LINK: http://www.powerlineblog.com/archives/2006/06/who-is-keith-ellison-9.php

[61] Brandt, Steve, "United for Peace Supporters Rally Against Police 'Power Grab'" Star Tribune, October 11, 1992. Link: https://www.newspapers.com/newspage/192700666/

[62] Reeves, Mel, "The Siege of Black Minneapolis" The Black Activist- Journal of the Black Left Unity Network, September 20, 2013. LINK: http://www.blackactivistzine.org/blackminneapolissieged.htm

[63] Reeves, Mel. "Ellison forced to the back of DNC bus," Minnesota Spokesman-Recorder, March 8, 2017. LINK: http://spokesman-recorder.com/2017/03/08/ellison-forced-back-dnc-bus/

[64] Hallman, Charles. "Too many people live in fear — summit aimed to quell street violence," Minnesota Spokesman-Recorder, June 20, 2017 LINK: http://spokesman-recorder.com/2017/06/20/peace-summit-aimed-quell-street-violence/

[65] Muller, Judy. "Victim's Son Helped Bring About SLA Arrests," ABC News, January 17, 2002 LINK: https://abcnews.go.com/WNT/story?id=130535&page=1

[66] NOTE: The other victim was Dr. Marcus A. Foster, Oakland superintendent, who was murdered on Election day 1973 (Foster's deputy superintendent Robert Blackburn was shot but survived after a "team of surgeons…worked all night to keep him alive.") "as they walked toward Blackburn's car at dusk after a school board meeting." They targeted Foster because of his perceived support of an identification card for students, that would be used to keep non-student drug dealers off campus. LINK: https://www.sfgate.com/bayarea/article/FORGOTTEN-FOOTNOTE-Before-Hearst-SLA-killed-2754621.php

[67] Federal Bureau of Investigation (FBI) website "A Byte Out of History: The Patty Hearst Kidnapping" Feb 4 2009 (archived) LINK: https://archives.fbi.gov/archives/news/stories/2009/february/hearst_020409

[68] Lopez, Steve. "A Son Has Been Waiting 26 Years for Justice," LA Times, January 17, 2002. LINK: http://articles.latimes.com/2002/jan/17/local/me-23183

[69] Fields-Meyer, Thomas. "Justice Delayed," People Magazine, March 11, 2002. LINK: http://people.com/archive/justice-delayed-vol-57-no-9/

[70] McLaughlin, Eliott C. "70s radical Sara Jane Olson released from prison," CNN, March 17, 2009. LINK: http://edition.cnn.com/2009/CRIME/03/17/olson.release/index.html?iref=nextin

[71] Staff Writer, "Olson Seeks to Raise Legal Defense Funds," Los Angeles Times, October 27, 1999 LINK: http://articles.latimes.com/1999/oct/27/local/me-26641

[72] Sara Olson Defense Committee; Keith Ellison's Speech UNGAGGED Forum held on February 12, 2000 (archived) LINK:

https://web.archive.org/web/20000823032901/http://www.saraolsondefense.com:80/Articles/Ungagged/Speech%20by%20Keith%20Ellison.html

73 Sara Olson Defense Committee; Peter Erlinder's Speech UNGAGGED Forum held on February 12, 2000 (archived) LINK: https://web.archive.org/web/20000823032914/http://www.saraolsondefense.com:80/Articles/Ungagged/Speech%20by%20Peter%20Erlinder.html

74 Murphy, Tim, "Keith Ellison Is Everything Republicans Thought Obama Was. Maybe He's Just What Democrats Need.," *Mother Jones*, March/April 2018 Issue, https://www.motherjones.com/politics/2017/02/keith-ellison-democratic-national-committee-chair/

75 Ibid

76 Williams, Brandt. "Jesse Jackson campaigns for Keith Ellison in Minneapolis" NPR News, June 30, 2006 LINK: https://www.mprnews.org/story/2006/06/30/jacksoncampaigns

77 Mother Jones

78 "Progressive for Congress comes under fire," People's World, August 11, 2006 LINK: http://www.peoplesworld.org/article/progressive-for-congress-comes-under-fire/

79 Marquit, Erwin CHAPTER 34. "CPUSA Enters 21st Century, and Jettisons the Gus Hall Stalinist Model of Party Organization," "Memoirs of a Lifelong Communist." (archived) 2000–2008 LINK: https://web.archive.org/web/20140516061447/http://www.tc.umn.edu/~marqu002/Chap34.pdf

80 Willkie, Phil. ""Keep working with me."—Congressman Keith Ellison," Pulse Twin Cities, April 18, 2007 (archived) LINK: https://web.archive.org/web/20160612154854/http://www.pulsetc.com/articlef192.html?op=Print&sid=3116

81 Ibid

82 Watne, John. "Rep. Ellison hosts house party," Examiner (archived) December 23, 2013 LINK: https://web.archive.org/web/20131227081501/http://www.examiner.com:80/article/rep-ellison-hosts-house-party

83 Ellison, Keith, "New grassroots movements show: Never count out working people," People's World, August 29, 2014 LINK: https://www.peoplesworld.org/article/new-grassroots-movements-show-never-count-out-working-people/

84 Ellison, Keith. "My Country, 'Tis of Thee: My Faith, My Family, Our Future," Page 140. Simon and Schuster, Oct 21, 2014

85 Democratic Socialists of America Publication List. "Cool Periodicals for the Literate Leftist" (archived); See screenshot LINK http://web.archive.org/web/19980626083306/http:/www.dsausa.org/rl/Links/Mags.html#DSAish

86 Staff, "911 Truth Statement Demands Deeper Investigation," October 26, 2004 LINK: http://911truth.org/911-truth-statement-demands-investigation/

[87] Kent State University, Special Collections and Archives "Information digest regarding the Seattle Liberation Front," LeRoy Satrom papers, May 2, 1970. LINK: https://omeka.library.kent.edu/special-collections/items/show/3390

[88] Democratic left, Jan./Feb. 1990, page 7 LINK FOR MORE DETAIL: https://keywiki.org/Jim_Scheibel

[89] City Hall Scoop with Tim Nelson & Jason Hoppin. "Look both ways: Ellison is coming," Twin Cities (Archived) August 04, 2006 LINK: https://web.archive.org/web/20070217215459/http://blogs.twincities.com:80/city_hall_scoop/2006/08/looks_like_the_.html

[90] Board of Directors, Wellstone Action as of June 30 2010 (archived) LINK: https://web.archive.org/web/20100613062146/http://www.wellstone.org/about-us/board-directors

[91] Reilly, Daniel W. "Sen. Wellstone's legacy lives on," Politico. October 25, 2007. LINK: https://www.politico.com/story/2007/10/sen-wellstones-legacy-lives-on-006543

[92] Loudon, Trevor, Keywiki Profile for Paul Wellstone, Compilation of DSA-related items with sources. LINK: https://keywiki.org/Paul_Wellstone

[93] Progressive Leadership Award, Midwest Academy (Archived) LINK: https://web.archive.org/web/20120721205857/http://www.midwestacademy.com/progressive-leadership-award

[94] Loudon, Trevor, Keywiki Profile for the Economic Policy Institute, Board Members are linked with sources. LINK: http://keywiki.org/Economic_Policy_Institute

[95] Official statements from the DSA's National Political Committee. "After the Ellison Defeat: Continuing the Struggle Against the Neoliberal Democratic Party Establishment" February 27, 2017 LINK: http://www.dsausa.org/statements?page=3

[96] Svart, Maria. "Remembering Tim Carpenter" dsausa.org, May 2, 2014 LINK: http://www.dsausa.org/remembering_tim_carpenter

[97] Carpenter, Tim. "Progressive Democrats of America--A New Organization Spreading Across the Country, Progressive Democrats of America, September 26, 2006 LINK: https://www.organicconsumers.org/news/progressive-democrats-america-new-organization-spreading-across-country

[98] Loudon, Trevor, Keywiki Profile for Tim Carpenter linked with sources. LINK: https://keywiki.org/Tim_Carpenter

[99] Progressive Democrats of America; "PDA Inside-Outside Strategy," Retrieved March 2007 (archived) LINK: https://web.archive.org/web/20070314155548/http://pdamerica.org/about/strategy.php

[100] Progressive Democrats of America; "Advisory Board" Retrieved March 2007 (archived) LINK: https://web.archive.org/web/20070317204205/http://pdamerica.org:80/about/board.php

[101] Powers-Hannley, Samantha. "PDA sponsors 'People's Inauguration' in DC on Jan 19: Watch live streaming," Blog for Arizona, Retrieved April 14, 2013 (archived) LINK:

https://web.archive.org/web/20130414221919/http://www.blogforarizona.com/blog/2013/01/pda-sponsors-peoples-inauguration-in-dc-on-jan-19-watch-live-streaming-.html

[102] PDA Advisory Board, accessed May 4, 2018 http://pdamerica.org/about-pda/advisory-board-members/

[103] Nichols, John. "Tim Carpenter's Politics of Radical Inclusion: In the Streets and in the Polling Booths," The Nation, April 29, 2014

[104] Democratic Socialists of America, Greater Detroit Local, "In the early 1970's, Democrat Ron Dellums, the left-wing congressman representing Berkeley and Oakland, joined the Democratic Socialist Organizing Committee, the group founded by legendary activist Michael Harrington with an explicit strategy of functioning openly as a socialist group within the Democratic Party." Past Newsletters, 2007. (archived) LINK: https://web.archive.org/web/20120629193234/http://kincaidsite.com/dsa/nl-archive.html

[105] Loudon, Trevor, Profile for Ron Dellums. Keywiki.org LINK: https://keywiki.org/Ron_Dellums

[106] Baiman, Ron. "Reorganized Illinois Citizen Action," New Ground 56, Jan-Feb 1998 (archived) LINK: https://web.archive.org/web/20020326111241/http://chicagodsa.org/ngarchive/ng56.html

[107] "About the Young Democratic Socialists of JMU," James Madison University, accessed May 19, 2010 (archived) LINK: https://web.archive.org/web/20151224042430/http://www.jmu.edu/orgs/youngdemsoc/aboutus.htm

[108] Democratic Socialists of America Greater Detroit Local, "The text above is based on a recent flyer from the national office of DSA" (archived) "LINK: https://web.archive.org/web/20111104084253/http://kincaidsite.com/dsa/

[109] CPUSA Report on the 2002 Elections, National Committee Meeting February 22, 2002, LINK: http://www.cpusa.org/article/report-on-the-2002-elections/

[110] Marquit, Erwin, "Contribution of the Communist Party USA, 14th International Meeting of CWP, member of International Department, CPUSA, Solidnet.org, 25 November 2012 LINK: http://www.solidnet.org/usa-communist-party-usa/14-imcwp-contribution-of-cpusa-en

[111] Wojcik, John. "Congressional Progressive Caucus introduces biggest jobs bill yet," People's World, December 13 2011 LINK: http://www.peoplesworld.org/article/congressional-progressive-caucus-introduces-biggest-jobs-bill-yet/

[112] Castro, Fidel. "The seven Congress members who are visiting us," Havana. April 7, 2009 (archived) LINK: https://web.archive.org/web/20090411103216/http://www.granma.cu/ingles/2009/april/mar7/Reflections-6april.html

[113] Marable, Manning. "Abolishing American Apartheid, Root and Branch," dialogue&initiative: Journal of Theory and Practice of the Committees of Correspondence Education Fund, Inc. winter 2003 edition (archived) LINK:

https://web.archive.org/web/20110218173633/https://www.cc-ds.org/pub_arch/dialogue_pdf/winter03mitchell.pdf

[114] Outlaws in Amerika, West Goals 1982, Pg 33-35

[115] Ellison, Keith. "My Country, 'Tis of Thee: My Faith, My Family, Our Future," Page 151. Simon and Schuster, Oct 21, 2014

[116] Zaman, Asad. LinkedIn, accessed April 13, 2018 LINK: https://www.linkedin.com/in/asadzaman/

[117] Middle East Forum, Islamist Watch, Money in Politics. https://www.meforum.org/islamist-watch/resources/islamist-money-in-politics

[118] Middle East Forum, "Islamist Watch: Money in Politics," "Keith Ellison," https://www.meforum.org/islamist-watch/resources/islamist-money-in-politics?recipientid=678&sort=date|asc&page=1

[119] Islamist Watch

[120] Center for Security Policy, "Star Spangled Shariah: The Rise of America's First Muslim Brotherhood Party," https://www.centerforsecuritypolicy.org/wp-content/uploads/2016/05/Star_Spangled_Shariah1.pdf

[121] Middle East Forum, "Islamist Watch: Money in Politics," "Keith Ellison," https://www.meforum.org/islamist-watch/resources/islamist-money-in-politics?recipientid=678&sort=date|asc&page=1

[122] Investigative Project on Terrorism, "North American Islamic Trust," http://www.investigativeproject.org/documents/misc/459.pdf

[123] Investigative Project on Terrorism, "North American Islamic Trust," http://www.investigativeproject.org/documents/misc/159.pdf

[124] Investigative Project on Terrorism, "FBI NAIT Investigation Indianapolis, IN," https://www.investigativeproject.org/activities/573/fbi-nait-investigation

[125] Investigative Project on Terrorism, "SAFA Group: Officers and Directors & Their Related Businesses and Organizations," https://www.investigativeproject.org/documents/case_docs/890.pdf

[126] Investigative Project on Terrorism, "SAAR Network: Herndon, Virginia," https://www.investigativeproject.org/activities/310/saar-network

[127] Muslim American Society Dossier, *The Investigative Project on Terrorism* http://www.investigativeproject.org/documents/misc/85.pdf

[128] Joseph Abrams, "Group That Funded Rep. Ellison's Pilgrimage to Mecca Called a Front for Extremism," Fox News, 8 January 2009. http://www.foxnews.com/politics/2009/01/08/group-funded-rep-ellisons-pilgrimage-mecca-called-extremism/

[129] Ibid

[130] Ellison, Keith. "My Country, 'Tis of Thee: My Faith, My Family, Our Future," Page 236-241. Simon and Schuster, Oct 21, 2014

[131] Star Tribune Islamic nonprofit paid for Rep. Ellison's pilgrimage to Mecca By KEVIN DIAZ Star Tribune JULY 22, 2009 LINK: http://www.startribune.com/islamic-nonprofit-paid-for-rep-ellison-s-pilgrimage/51361722/

[132] Scher, Brent. "Muslim Brotherhood-tied group paid for Keith Ellison to visit Mecca in 2008" Washington Free Beacon, November 22, 2016 LINK: http://www.foxnews.com/politics/2016/11/22/muslim-brotherhood-tied-group-paid-for-keith-ellison-to-visit-mecca-in-2008.html

[133] Zaman, Imam Asad, Facebook Posted December 29, 2017. LINK: https://www.facebook.com/photo.php?fbid=1599805036773391&set=ecnf.100002317296426&type=3&theater

[134] Ellison, Keith. "My Country, 'Tis of Thee: My Faith, My Family, Our Future," Page 236-241. Simon and Schuster, Oct 21, 2014

[135] SOP Newswire, "N.C. State Senator Larry Shaw Elected CAIR Board Chair" Student Operated Press, March 3rd, 2009 LINK: http://thesop.org/story/usa/2009/03/03/nc-state-senator-larry-shaw-elected-cair-board-chair.php

[136] The Council on American-Islamic Relations (CAIR): CAIR Exposed, *The Investigative Project on Terrorism*, http://www.investigativeproject.org/documents/misc/122.pdf; also see C.A.I.R. Is Hamas: How the Federal Government Proved that the Council on American-Islamic Relations is a front for Terrorism, *Center for Security Policy*, http://www.centerforsecuritypolicy.org/wp-content/uploads/2016/12/CAIR_is_HAMAS.pdf

[137] CAIR "Vision, Mission, Core Principles," October 01, 2015 LINK: http://www.cair.com/about-us/vision-mission-core-principles.html

[138] IPT News. "DOJ Seen Nothing Which 'Exonerates' CAIR," Investigative Project on Terrorism, Mar 26, 2010 LINK: https://www.investigativeproject.org/1875/doj-seen-nothing-which-exonerates-cair

[139] "Durbin's Flawed Hearing," Investigative Project on Terrorism, March 28, 2011 LINK: https://www.investigativeproject.org/2719/durbin-flawed-hearing

[140] IPT News. "CAIR's Awad: In support of the Hamas Movement," Investigative Project on Terrorism, March 22, 1994 LINK: https://www.investigativeproject.org/223/cairs-awad-in-support-of-the-hamas-movement

[141] Argiris Malapanis and Roman Kane. "World Youth Federation Meets In S. Africa," The Militant, October 23, 1995 LINK: http://www.themilitant.com/1995/5939/5939_13.html; Also see LINK: https://en.wikipedia.org/wiki/World_Federation_of_Democratic_Youth#Member_organization

[142] Awad, Nihad. Speaker at Act Now to Stop War and End Racism (A.N.S.W.E.R.) (A front group for the Workers World Party, which was later taken in a split in 2006 by Party of Socialism and Liberation and continues to this day.) Rally against Israel LINK: https://www.c-span.org/video/?169675-1/international-answer-rally&start=6379APRIL

[143] Awad, Nihad. Speaker at Act Now to Stop War and End Racism (A.N.S.W.E.R.) (A front group for the Party of Socialism and Liberation) Rally against Israel

LINK: https://www.c-span.org/video/?320825-1/rally-israeli-violence-gaza&start=2078; http://keywiki.org/Party_for_Socialism_and_Liberation

[144] ICP Newsroom, American socialists' ANSWER to Trump," International Communist Press, 23 January 2017 LINK: http://icp.sol.org.tr/americana/american-socialists-answer-trump

[145] Schwartz, Jessica. "Tampa event opposes U.S. war and political repression," FightBack! News, February 23, 2015 LINK: http://www.fightbacknews.org/2015/2/23/tampa-event-opposes-us-war-and-political-repression

[146] Joye, Barbara. "Resisting the Trump/Republican Agenda," Democratic Socialists of America, March 21, 2017 LINK: https://www.dsa-atlanta.org/resisting_the_trump_republican_agenda

[147] Najjab, Jamal. "CAIR Holds 12th Annual Fund-Raising Banquet," Washington Report on Middle East Affairs LINK: https://www.wrmea.org/007-january-february/muslim-american-activism-cair-holds-12th-annual-fund-raising-banquet.html

[148] CAIR California, SF Valley Community Event a Success, Rep. Keith Ellison gave a Keynote Address on "Defending our Democracy" Jun 02, 2011 (archived) LINK: https://web.archive.org/web/20110608083612/https://ca.cair.com/losangeles/news/sf_valley_event

[149] Rosenthal, Emma. "Zionist Campaign Against Free Speech: Corporate Funded Privatized Espionage," October 19, 2006 LINK: https://cafeintifada.wordpress.com/2006/10/19/corporate-funded-privatized-espionage/

[150] Press Release: "Sold-Out CAIR-MN Annual Banquet a Success," CAIR Minnesota website, 16 April 2013 LINK: http://mn.cair.com/media/press-releases/157-sold-out-cair-mn-annual-banquet-a-success.html,

[151] CAIR. "WATCH: New CAIR ISLAMOPHOBIN Ad 'Crushes' Islamophobia," July 25, 2016 LINK: https://www.cair.com/press-center/press-releases/13669-watch-new-cair-islamophobin-ad-crushes-islamophobia.html

[152] Getty Images, "Congressman Keith Ellison speaks during a dining and discussion event," 2 March 2016 https://www.gettyimages.com/detail/news-photo/congressman-keith-ellison-speaks-during-a-dining-and-news-photo/513450686#congressman-keith-ellison-speaks-during-a-dining-and-discussion-event-picture-id513450686

[153] Hena Zuberi, "Leaders Say Coordinating Council Needed for Muslims of the Western World," The Muslim Link, 21 February 2016 http://www.muslimlinkpaper.com/community-news/4106leaders-say-coordinating-council-needed-for-muslims-of-the-western-world

[154] Yasin Aktay, "Greetings and a message from Western Muslims," Yeni Şafak, 6 February 2016 https://web.archive.org/web/20160211043643/http://www.yenisafak.com/en/columns/yasinaktay/greetings-and-a-message-from-western-muslims-2026; https://www.yenisafak.com/en/columns/yasinaktay/greetings-and-a-message-from-western-muslims-2026629?n=1

[155] Steven Emerson and John Rossomando. "Dems Tap Radical Islamists for Cash," Investigative Project on Terrorism, November 1, 2012 LINK: https://www.investigativeproject.org/3792/dems-tap-radical-islamists-for-cash

[156] Stern, Jacob. "Sen. Chris Murphy visits Elm City" Yale News, February 6, 2017 LINK: https://yaledailynews.com/blog/2017/02/06/murphy-visits-elm-city/

[157] Cukurova, Gokhan. "The American Communist," (Archived May 21, 2016) LINK: https://web.archive.org/web/20160521144757/http://www.gokhan.us:80/the-american-communist

[158] Loudon, Trevor. "Security Risk: Meet Senator Chris Murphy's long-time Communist Party USA staffer," Canada Free Press, July 8, 2017 LINK: https://canadafreepress.com/article/security-risk-meet-senator-chris-murphys-long-time-communist-party-usa-staf

[159] National Muslim Democratic Council Secret Flyer LINK: https://www.investigativeproject.org/documents/misc/726.pdf

[160] "Washington Report on Middle East Affairs; Human Rights On the Ground in Gaza," April 2009, page 47 LINK: https://www.wrmea.org/2009-april/on-the-ground-in-gaza.html

[161] "Ellison, McCollum and Oberstar urge Obama to lift Gaza blockade," The Minnesota Independent, Jan. 26, 2010 (archived) LINK: https://web.archive.org/web/20110918224308/http://minnesotaindependent.com/54474/ellison-oberstar-and-mccollum-urge-lifting-of-gaza-blockade

[162] Hocaoglu, Fatma, "ONE"YEAR"AFTER" "OPERATION"CAST"LEAD" No"Change," No"Accountability," Muslim Public Affairs Council, January 2010 (archived) LINK: https://web.archive.org/web/20100211000438/http://www.mpac.org/docs/Gaza-One-Year-After.pdf

[163] Gulf News Staff, "Qatar speech questions Ellison's affiliation" By Gulf News Journal Reports, Dec 11, 2016 LINK: https://gulfnewsjournal.com/stories/511056100-qatar-speech-questions-ellison-s-affiliation

[164] Press release, "Pelosi, Congressional Delegation Arrive in Egypt," March 14, 2012. LINK: https://www.democraticleader.gov/newsroom/pelosi-congressional-delegation-arrive-egypt/

[165] Ellison, Keith. "My Country, 'Tis of Thee: My Faith, My Family, Our Future," Page 267. Simon and Schuster, Oct 21, 2014

[166] Democratic Left Issue 1998, page 6

[167] Arena Profile: James J. Zogby, Politico, LINK: http://www.politico.com/arena/bio/james_j_zogby.html

[168] Dinan, Stephen. "Obama climate czar has socialist ties," Washington Times, January 12, 2009 LINK: https://www.washingtontimes.com/news/2009/jan/12/obama-climate-czar-has-socialist-ties/

[169] 8th Socialist Scholars Conference, April 6-8, 1990, conference program LINK: https://keywiki.org/Socialist_Scholars_Conference_1990

[170] Stein, Jeff. "Bernie Sanders moved Democrats to the left. The platform is proof." Vox, Jul 25, 2016 LINK: https://www.vox.com/2016/7/25/12281022/the-democratic-party-platform

[171] Rep. Keith Ellison Slams Amazon for Selling 'Hate Group' Merchandise, by Renae Reints, Fortune magazine, July 17, 2018. LINK: http://fortune.com/2018/07/17/keith-ellison-jeff-bezos-letter/

Index

1

14th International Meeting of Communist and Workers Parties, 52

2

21st Century Democrats, 43

9

9/11 Truther, 43

A

Abbas, Roxanne, 20
Abdul-Samad, Rep. Ako, 66
Adams, Jamiah, 71
AFCSME, 74
Africana Student Cultural Center, 10
Ahmadinejad, Mahmoud, 19, 103
Ahmed, Omar, 63
AK Party, 67
Akhter, Assad, 71
Aktay, Yasin, 67, 111
Al Rajhi, Sulaiman Abdul Aziz, 59
Ali, Saqib, 65
Alinsky, Saul, 7, 44
All Dulles Area Muslim Society (ADAMS) Center, 59
All-African People's Revolutionary Party, 24
Allen, George, 70
al-Qaeda, 59
Al-Taqwa Bank, 69
American Civil Liberties Union (ACLU), 61
American Friends Service Committee, 66
American Indian Movement, 27
American Jewish World, 35
American Muslims for Palestine (AMP), 58
American Prospect, The, 44
Andrews, Tom, 50
Arab American Association of New York, 66, 71
Arneson, Nancy, 38, 40
Asbahi, Mazen, 70, 71
Awad, Nihad, 59, 63, 64, 66, 67, 69, 82, 110
Ayloush, Hussam, 65

B

Badawi, Samer, 72
Barzinji, Jamal, 59, 69
Beatty, Joyce, 71
Beirut, Lebanon, 52
Bellecourt, Clyde, 27
Ben Mohammad al-Qasmini, Sultan, Sheik, 9
Benjamin, Medea, 48
Bey El-Amin, Abdullah, 9
Black American Law Students Association, 16
Black Left Unity Network, 29, 105
Black Panther Party, 24
Black Student Union, 7
Bond, Julian, 44
Booth, Paul, 74
Bowles, Shannon, 28, 29
Brandt, Steve, 29, 105, 106
Browner, Carol, 74

C

Carmichael, Stokely. *See* Ture, Kwame
Carpenter, Tim, 47, 49, 107, 108

Carson, Andre, 9, 10, 14, 69, 70, 101
Castro, Fidel, 54
Castro, Julian, 18
Center for American Progress, 74
Central Intelligence Agency (CIA), 78
China, 24, 37, 44, 55, 61, 64, 65
Chisholm, Shirley, 54
Clinton, Bill, 9, 17, 103
Clinton, Hillary, 74
Cohn, Marjorie, 48
Committee in Solidarity with the People of Syria, 19
Committees of Correspondence for Democracy and Socialism, 55
Communist Party USA, 7, 25, 36, 37, 42, 51, 52, 70, 108, 112
Communist Party USA (CPUSA), 36, 37, 40, 41, 52, 106, 108
Communist Workers Party, 55, 65
Congressional Black Caucus (CBC), 25, 52, 54, 55, 83
Congressional Hispanic Caucus, 52
Congressional Progressive Caucus, 39, 42, 47, 49, 50, 51, 52, 53, 108
Conyers, John, 7, 25, 47, 48, 54, 101, 104
Costain, Pam, 57
Council on American Islamic Relations (CAIR), 59, 62, 63, 64, 65, 66, 67, 69, 70, 71, 81, 82, 83, 84, 110, 111
Council on American-Islamic Relations (CAIR), 58
Crockett, George, 7, 101
Cuba, 22
Cummings, Elijah, 65
Curbelo, Frank, 23

D

Darrow, Clarence, 7, 101
Day, Corey, 36
DeFazio, Peter, 50
Dellums, Ron, 50, 54, 108

Democratic Congressional Campaign Committee, 69
Democratic Left Magazine, 47
Democratic National Committee (DNC), 6, 30, 44, 50, 75
Democratic Party, 36, 37, 39, 45, 47, 49, 51, 52, 54, 69, 70, 73, 74, 75, 103, 107, 108
Democratic Socialists of America (DSA), 43, 44, 46, 47, 50, 55, 64, 71, 74, 106, 108, 111
Department of Homeland Security, 60
Department of Justice, 58, 60, 70
Detroit Free Press, 7
Doha, Qatar, 72
Dohrn, Bernadine, 32
Dowd, Jeff Alan, 43
DSA. *See* Democratic Socialists of America

E

Economic Policy Institute, 107
Edwards, Donna, 48
Egypt, 9, 72, 73, 112
Eker, Mehmet Mehdi, 62
Electronic Intifada, 65
Elkarra, Basim, 71
Ellison, Clida, 6
Ellison, Isaiah, 20
Ellison, Kim, 30
Ellison, Leonard Sr., 6
El-Sadat, Anwar, 9
El-Shabazz, Adl, 28
Embassy Suites Five, 18
Erdogan, Recep Tayyip, 62, 66, 67
Erlinder, Peter, 32
Evans, Lane, 50

F

Falwell, Sandy, 48
Fanon, Frantz, 7
Farrakhan, Louis, 9, 10, 11, 13, 14, 102

Farrakhan, Mustapha, 14
Faux, Jeff, 44
Federal Bureau of Investigation (FBI), 11, 20, 21, 22, 59, 63, 65, 77, 78, 103, 105, 109
Fight Back!, 21
Fishman, Joelle, 52
Fletcher, Jr., Bill, 48
Ford, Jr., A.C., 28
Forward Motion, 16
Freedom Road Socialist Organization, 16, 19, 20, 48, 64
Fuerzas Armadas Revolucionarias de Colombia (FARC), 21

G

General Union of Palestinian Students, 64
Gerard, Leo, 44
Ghilarducci, Teresa, 44
Golden Chain, 59
Goldman, Max, 70
Goold, Bill, 47
Grafton, Rev. Dr. David D., 66
Granma (Cuba Communist Party Journal), 54
Greene, Marion, 40
Grijalva, Raul, 48, 49, 50, 52, 53
Guantanamo Bay, 73
Gunnels, Warren, 74
Gutierrez, Luis, 74

H

Haaf, Jerry, 27, 28, 32, 104
Hahn, Geoff, 16
Hakim, Keith E., 10
HAMAS, 58, 60, 62, 63, 64, 66, 67, 110
Hanlon, Stuart, 32
Hard Times Conference, 57
Harris, Ed, 28, 29
Harris, Emily Montague, 30
Havana, 24
Hawkins, Augustus, 54

Hayden, Tom, 48
Hearst, Patty, 30
Hearst, William Randolph, 31
Herrera, Nachito, 23
Herzallah, Taher, 59
Hoekstra, Pete, 70
Holder, Eric, 21
Holets, Dave, 38
Holy Land Foundation, 58, 62, 64, 70
Honda, Mike, 65
Hoover, J. Edgar, 78
Hornstein, Frank, 57

I

IKHWAN (Muslim Brotherhood), 59
Indonesia, 61
Institute for Policy Studies, 22, 23, 46, 48
International Association of Democratic Lawyers, 48
International Institute of Islamic Thought (IIIT), 58, 59
Investigative Project on Terrorism, 59, 63, 109, 110, 112
Iosbaker, Joe, 19, 21
Iqbal, Zeba, 71
Iraq, 20, 35, 37, 39, 47, 73
Islamic Circle of North America (ICNA), 58, 59, 62, 82
Islamic Society of North America (ISNA), 58, 59, 82, 83, 84
Israel, Steve, 69

J

Jackson Lee, Sheila, 65
Jackson, Jesse, 36, 74, 106
Jaka, Rizwan, 59
Jammal, Oussama (USCMO Secretary General), 58, 67
Jarrar, Raed, 66
Jewish Voice for Peace, 66
Johnson, Scott, 29, 30

Jordan, Susan, 33

K

Kaine, Tim, 70
Kane, David, 60
Kansas City, 30
Kaspari, Dick, 57
Kelly, Joseph H., 43
Kerry, John, 41, 72
King, Jr., Dr. Martin Luther, 48
Klobuchar, Amy, 66
Knutson, April, 37, 38
Knutson, Jim, 38
Krohnke, Duane W., 23
Kunstler, William, 7, 101
Kushner, Jordan, 16, 39, 66
Kuttner, Robert, 44

L

League of Revolutionary Struggle, 44
Lee, Barbara, 48
Legal Rights Center, 27
Lerner, Rabbi Michael, 43
Lighty, Michael, 48
Lugg, Amanda, 48
Lutheran Theological Seminary, 66

M

Maloney, Carolyn, 73
Marable, Manning, 55
Marcantonio, Vito, 78
Markey, Ed, 73
Marquit, Doris, 37
Marquit, Erwin, 37
Marshall, Chip, 43
Martin, Sarah, 19
Marzook, Mousa Abu, 63
McDermott, Jim, 72
McGovern, Jim, 47
McGrath, Dan, 57
McInerney, Denise, 15
McKenzie, Mwati (Pepi), 28

Mecca, 57, 60, 61, 62, 83, 109, 110
Meeks, Gregory, 14
Mgeni, Yusef, 17
Midwest Academy, 44, 107
Militant Forum, 15
Militant, The, Socialist Workers Party publication, 15, 17, 102, 103, 110
Million Man March, 10, 11, 12, 13, 17
Minneapolis, 11, 15, 16, 19, 20, 22, 23, 27, 28, 29, 30, 35, 36, 38, 39, 42, 81, 102, 104, 105, 106
Minneapolis City Council, 15
Minnesota Board of Teaching, 57
Minnesota Cuba Committee, 23
Minnesota Daily, 10
Minnesota Peace Project, 20, 103
Minnesota Rabbi Imam Round Table, 57
Mirza, Yaqub, 59
Mishel, Larry, 44
Mitchell, Parren, 54
Mohammed, Warith Deen, 9, 101
Molm, Tracy, 21
Moore, Ty, 39
Moss, Spike, 13
Mother Jones, 7, 11, 18, 35, 36, 101, 106
Muhammad, Abdul Akbar, 14
Muhammad, Elijah, 9
Muhammed, Khalid, 11
Murphy, Chris, 70
Murphy, Patrick, 70
Murphy, Tim, 11, 18
Muslim American Society, 57, 58, 60, 61, 62, 82, 83, 84, 109
Muslim American Society of Minnesota, The, 57, 61
Muslim Brotherhood, 58, 59, 60, 62, 63, 66, 67, 69, 73, 81, 84, 109, 110
Muslim Center, 9
Muslim Public Affairs Council (MPAC), 58, 72, 82, 83

Muslim Student Association, 69

N

NAACP, 6, 17
Nada, Youssef, 69
Nation of Islam, 9, 10, 11, 13, 14, 104
National Conference of Black Lawyers, 33
National Lawyers Guild, 32, 57
National Muslim Democratic Council, 69, 70, 112
National Nurses United, 48
National Urban Peace & Justice Summit, 30
Nevel, Donna, 66
New School for Social Research, The, 44
Nimtz, August, 3, 17, 23, 24, 35, 103
Nisan, Chris, 16
Noguera, Pedro, 44
North American Islamic Trust (NAIT), 58, 59, 109
North Vietnam, 24

O

Obama, Barack, 21, 22, 23, 41, 52, 53, 70, 72, 73, 74, 101, 106, 112
Olson, Deborah, 44
Olson, Sara Jane. *See* Kathleen Soliah
Omeish, Esam, 59
Operation Green Quest, 60
Opsahl, Myrna, 30, 31

P

Pakistan, 61
Palestine Committee, 63
Palestine Liberation Organization (PLO), 64
Palestinian Islamic Jihad, 60, 69, 82, 83

Party for Socialism and Liberation, 64
Paymar, Michael, 44
Pelosi, Nancy, 39, 69, 73, 82
People's World, Communist Party USA newspaper, 37, 106, 108
Perez, Tom, 44
Persichini, Joseph, Jr., 65
Piven, Frances Fox, 44
Popular Front for the Liberation of Palestine, 21
Prairie Fire Organizing Committee, 57
Pratt, Geronimo jiJaga, 33
Progressive Democrats of America, 46, 47, 48, 49, 107
Progressive Student Network, 16
Progressive Student Organization, 66

Q

Qatar, 72

R

Rahall, Nick, 73
Rainbow Coalition, 36, 74
Rangel, Charles B., 54
Rashad, Kameelah M., 66
Reeves, Mel, 29
ReThink Media, 59
Robin Hood Tax, 48, 49
Rosenthal, Vic, 57
Rouhani, Hassan, 14

S

SAAR Network (SAFA Group), 59, 60, 109
Sabo, Martin, 35
Sadler, Rev. Rodney, 48
SAFA Group. *See* SAAR Network
Said, Jamal, 70
Sanders, Bernie, 45, 46, 50, 51, 73, 74, 113

Sarfehjooy, Margaret, 20
Sarsour, Linda, 66, 71
Saylor, Corey, 59
Scheibel, Jim, 43, 44
Seattle Liberation Front, 43
Shabazz, Qubilah, 11
Shamsud-Din, Mitchell, 9
Shariah, 59
Shaw, Larry, 62
Sheehan, Cindy, 48
Sincere and Loyal African American Men (SALAAM), 10
Sinema, Kyrsten, 48
Socialist Alternative, 39
Socialist International, 74
Socialist Workers Party, 24
Soliah, Kathleen, 31
South End (student newspaper), 7
Stabenow, Debbie, 70
Student Nonviolent Coordinating Committee (SNCC), 24
Sunni Islam, 9, 57
Svart, Maria, 46
Symbionese Liberation Army (SLA), 30
Syria, 19

T

Tanden, Neera, 74
Tarek ibn Ziyad Academy (TiZA), 61
The City, Inc., 28
Together We Serve, 59
Ture, Kwame, 24, 25, 43
Turkey, 67

U

United Arab Emirates, 9
United for Peace, 28, 29, 30, 105
United Nations Relief and Works Agency (UNRWA), 72
United Nations, The, 36, 72
United Palestinian Appeal, 72
United States Council of Muslim Organizations (USCMO), 58, 59, 60, 66, 67, 84
United States Council of Muslim Organizations, The (USCMO), 58, 59, 66, 84
University of Minnesota Law School, 15, 24
Urban Coalition, 17

V

Vice Lords, 27, 28

W

Washington, Kimberly, 15
Wasserman Schultz, Debbie, 74
Wayne State University, 6, 9
Weather Underground, 32, 43, 57
Wellstone, Paul, 20, 35, 37, 44, 107
West, Allen, 70
West, Dr. Cornel, 73
Whitley, Andrew, 72
Williams, Jihad, 71
Willis, Monterey, 28
Willis, Sharif, 27, 28, 29, 30
Women Against Military Madness (WAMM), 19, 20, 103
Workers World Party, 64, 110
World Federation of Democratic Youth (WFDY), 64

Y

Young Democratic Socialists (James Madison University), 51

Z

Zaman, Asad, 57, 60, 61, 62, 83
Zogby, James, 74